Caribbean
Popular
Culture

Caribbean Popular Culture

Edited
by
John A. Lent

Bowling Green State University Popular Press
Bowling Green, Ohio 43403

Copyright ©1990 by Bowling Green State University Popular Press

Library of Congress Catalogue Card No.: 90-83084

ISBN: 087972-499-4 cb
     087972-500-1 pb

Cover design by Laura Darnell-Dumm

To Frank Manning, a pioneer, who intimately knew and loved Caribbean popular culture

Contents

Preface

John A. Lent

Popular culture in the Caribbean has been grossly understudied. Only recently have universities of the region (and elsewhere) produced a limited number of scholars and students who have done systematic research on the field of study. And, although the literature review of Chapter One contains many citations, until now, there has not been between two covers an overview of different Caribbean popular culture forms.

As indicated in the first chapter, this deficiency may be attributed to the lack of definition of the field and to academic snobbery. Other reasons may be offered: 1. When scholars finally recognized the region as being worthy of study, they were too consumed by more pressing economic and political issues to be bothered by popular culture; 2. Popular culture, a newly-recognized discipline in North America and Europe, is even newer in the Caribbean and, therefore, has not generated a body of specialists; 3. Those involved in popular culture pursuits in the Caribbean were too preoccupied "doing" it, to take time out to study it.

The compilation of these essays attempts to redress part of this shortcoming; it touches upon several genres of different linguistic and cultural settings and is written by scholars, some of whom have had long-term commitments to popular culture, others new to the field. Included here are chapters discussing Carnival, music, radio drama and other radio fare, and sports. Countries featured in case studies are Trinidad and Tobago, Antigua, U.S. Virgin Islands, Martinique, Guadeloupe, and Jamaica; research techniques employed are participant-observation, interviewing, content analysis, and structural analysis.

Common themes stand out in some of the contributions. One that predominates is that of cultural imperialism and/or dependency. In her chapter on Guadeloupe's Radyo Tanbou, Ruprecht makes the point that the station uses an "ideological position" to fight French colonialism and dependency. She shows how the station presents both sides of controversial issues, using a "we" and "they" dichotomy.

1

Treitler and de Albuquerque also take up the cultural imperialism theme in their depiction of Antiguan and U.S. Virgin Islands' Carnival. In Antigua, Carnival has evolved into two divisions—the performance tents, attended usually by tourists, and Las Vegas, mainly reserved for locals. According to Treitler, the latter is where one finds the local cultural artifacts. De Albuquerque, in his study of U.S. Virgin Islands' Carnival, provides a picture of the tensions experienced when local people believe they are losing their grasp of a local cultural form.

Taking an opposite perspective, the Mandles contend that although basketball players in Trinidad and Tobago view many National Basketball Association games via satellite-relayed television, and imitate styles of play and individual performances, they are not doing so because of cultural imperialism. Manning shows the adaptations made when the Caribbean cultural form Carnival is exported to other countries.

A second theme concentrates on the grassroots involvement in some of these popular culture genres. The Mandles emphasize the penetration of basketball to the remotest areas, while Ruprecht tells how Radyo Tanbou caters to the common folk, soliciting their viewpoints over the air and using their dialect, rather than French, in broadcasts. Hazzard and Cambridge portray some of Elaine Perkins' developmental soap operas as being built around make-believe villages, using characters normally associated with them, in an effort to communicate with real-life villagers. Guilbault treats *zouk* as a music form popular among the masses.

Present in a few of these essays is the message that popular culture, such as Carnival, but also calypso, reggae, and Radyo Tanbou, serve as outlets for the pent-up frustrations of the poor, allowing them to experience, though momentarily and vicariously, a better lifestyle.

Some essays discuss uses made of popular culture for political and developmental purposes. Wilson studies the impact of reggae bandwagon music upon the 1972 Jamaican election, claiming it helped sweep Michael Manley into office; Hazzard and Cambridge relate how a radio soap opera was employed to promote family planning, and Ruprecht describes a radio station's push for national independence and identity.

Cuthbert and Wilson discuss ways that Jamaican musicians have been exploited. Interviewing a number of the reggae performers, they found that internationally, their music was "stolen" from them; domestically, they were pawns of radio disc jockeys who demanded payola.

The book begins with an overview, citing representative literature, followed by three chapters on Carnival, three on various music forms, two on radio, and ending with a chapter on sports. Except for those of Chapter One, all references are placed at the end of the volume. Because the first chapter is a literature review, the references are kept nearby.

Chapter One
Popular Culture in the Caribbean:
A Literature Review

John A. Lent

Caribbean popular culture has made the international scene, in recent years, as Africans, Europeans, and North Americans dance to the rhythm of reggae, cheer on world—famous West Indian cricket or baseball players, and party at overseas versions of Carnival. Occasionally, they may listen to commercialized calypso, read a novel, play, or short story of one of the many Caribbean literary geniuses, or take in a Cuban film at an art theater.

Corresponding to this internationalization has been the development of a field of study among scholars. However, the study of Caribbean popular culture, much like that of the field generally, has been very recent, uneven—some artifacts receiving much attention while others go unnoticed—,scattered, fragmented, and tentative.

Reasons for this state of affairs can be found in the diversity of backgrounds of those researching the field, in the academic snobbery, and in the definition of popular culture itself. Anthropologists, economists, journalists, ethnomusicologists, historians, sociologists, among others, have contributed to the literature. These different approaches to the subject are, no doubt, beneficial, but with so many disciplines involved, popular culture specialists remain "academic boat people," drifting about without a home.

Popular culture has not been studied often and well because of the eliteness of academic communities, usually repulsed by objects of mass culture, or at least pretending to be. As Lewis (1979, p. 35) wrote, only "recently, and grudgingly" have social scientists in the United States and Europe conceded that contemporary culture is worth studying. Popular culture has been dumped on the same academic trash heap occupied by mass communications and information a generation or more ago. Social scientists "discovered" the importance of mass communications in their studies only after governmental, business, and other interests put up the money for research; perhaps the same motivator will be needed for popular culture.

Lewis (1979, p. 36) provided four major criticisms of popular culture used by the academic community as justifications for ignoring it. They are: 1. negative character of popular culture creation—undesirable because it is mass-produced by profit—motivated entrepreneurs for the gratification of a paying audience; 2. negative effects on high culture through borrowing and eventual debasement; 3. negative effects on the popular culture audience with spurious, and sometimes emotionally harmful, gratification; 4. negative effects on society through wide distribution channels which reduce the level of cultural quality.

Probably most detrimental has been the confusion associated with trying to define popular culture. Complaining that it has too many meanings and too little theory and classification, Lewis (1979, p. 40) said:

Thus, one has labelled as popular culture peasant art in Yugoslavia, folk dance in Nigeria, working class culture in Elizabethan England, Pompeian graffiti, contemporary rock music, Mexican—American barrio wall murals, and the products of Walt Disney.

In his own efforts to delineate the field, Lewis used subcategories of mass, folk, and elite cultures. He believed popular culture should not be limited to the study of industrialized societies, but also folk-based, traditional ones. Elite culture, he said, is usually not of popular culture, but defined within the popular culture context (Lewis 1979:41). Popular culture in the Caribbean will be broadly categorized because of these unclear and inconsistent definitions.

A number of questions are left unanswered when dealing with Caribbean popular culture. How does one categorize Caribbean folk forms that become popular? With all the superimpositions of cultures in the region, what is Caribbean popular culture, as distinguished from U.S., British, French, Dutch, or Spanish popular cultures? Where is the cut—off point between mass communications and popular culture, or is there one?

In this literature review, advertising, television, or magazines, although they play large roles in Caribbean popular culture, will be omitted. Studies of these and other mass communication forms can be found in abundance elsewhere. Film and comic art, however, are included because they are integral parts of popular culture. Also included are music, carnival, and sports. This review is more representative than it is exhaustive.

General Resources

Besides sources on Caribbean mass communications (Lent 1977, 1981; Cuthbert and Pidgeon 1981; Brown and Sanatan 1987; Soderlund and Surlin 1985) that are very useful to the study of popular culture, other more specific materials also exist.

Much of it appears in the periodical literature, including an annual dealing with popular culture in Latin America and the Caribbean. Initiated at the beginning of the 1980s, the well-edited *Studies in Latin American Popular Culture* is thick with articles of relevance. Other popular culture journals, including the *Journal of Popular Culture* and other periodicals of Bowling Green University's Popular Press, and the now—defunct *International Popular Culture*, have carried occasional articles, as have area studies periodicals such as *Caribbean Review, Caribbean Quarterly, Jamaica Journal, Caribbean Contact*, and the many periodicals of Cuba and the Dominican Republic.

Cuba is most developed of Caribbean nations in the production of periodical literature on popular culture. *Cine Cubano*, in over 115 issues since it was started in 1960, has done a splendid job of documenting Cuban, and to a lesser extent, Latin American, film. It has had scores of interviews with prominent directors, such as Alvarez, Solás, García Espinosa, Gutierrez Alea, and Goméz, as well as reviews and essays on films. Photography is discussed in *Fototecnica*, journalism in *UPEC* and *CEMEDIM*, and sports in *Semanario Deportivo LPV*, which dates to the 1960s. Additionally, Cuban institutions regularly publish journals for literature, theater, and dance.

In Jamaica, the *Journal of West Indian Literature* was initiated in 1987 by the University of the West Indies (see review in *Caribbean Contact*, June 1987: 10-11).

Longer treatments discussing Caribbean culture in general terms include Nettleford (1979) and two in a UNESCO series, "Studies and Documents on Cultural Policies." Nettleford covered all popular cultural genres, including theater, dance, music, film, painting, mass media, and sports, placing them in the context of their use for development and social change. The UNESCO documents dealt with Cuba and Jamaica and were published in the late 1970s. They discussed cultural associations, their objectives and budgets, and other information in light of national cultural policy.

Taylor (1989) explored roles of written and oral traditions in Caribbean peoples' struggles for identity and self-determination. He particularly scanned the narrative of Frantz Fanon, but also those of Haitian *Vandou* and Jamaican *Anancy* trickster tales.

Carnival

A number of popular culture forms are identified with Carnival; among these are calypso, 'mas (masquerade bands), and steel band. A product of Trinidad, Carnival in recent times has been exported as one of that country's major products, to smaller Caribbean countries, Canada, England, and the U.S. At the same time, it has become highly commercialized.

Relative to its significance, Carnival has not been researched extensively. Hill (1972) and Boyke (1973) wrote books on Carnival in Trinidad and Tobago; the latter featured among other essays, one by the calypsonian, "The Mighty Sparrow." Others have explored smaller-island carnivals: Abrahams (1970), Tobago; Crowley (1955), St. Lucia, and Abrahams and Bauman (1978), St. Vincent. The latter island was also featured in *Carnival: St. Vincent and the Grenadines* (n.d.). *Caribbean Quarterly* devoted its fourth issue of 1956 to Carnival in Trinidad and the rest of the region. Crowley (1956) studied traditional Carnival masques, and Pearse (1956) did a historical appraisal of Trinidadian Carnival in the nineteenth century. Pearse's work was based on Trinidadian newspaper accounts of Carnival. Belizean Carnival was written about by Briceño (1981).

Manning (1978), who has written more on Caribbean popular culture than nearly any other scholar, observed Antiguan Carnival, showing how it differed from that of Trinidad. He said Antigua's Carnival had more emblems of island identity, regional harmony, and themes of black identity, and is held in August.

Some writers have concentrated on overseas Carnival, established by West Indians in New York, London, Toronto, Montreal, and to a lesser degree elsewhere in the U.S. All described the difficulties in setting up Carnival because of class, race, and island differences. Manning (1983a) said Toronto Carnival, a year-round affair—whenever Caribbean people get together, has distinctly Canadian characteristics. Cohen (1980, 1982) found similar political splits associated with the creation of a London Carnival.

Discussing exportation of the Carnival industry, Manning (1983b) said it has moved from populists roots ("we ting") to the "Greatest Show on Earth," with significant changes in its artistic and commercial organization. For example, masquerade bands have become bigger and more spectacular, and more costly, making them a middle—class hobby that is out of the reach of many former participants. Steel bands no longer play a big role in island Carnival, according to Manning, because their music is inaudible in the streets (because of modern sound systems), and calypso has been replaced by soca (simpler lyrics and heavier baseline rhythm), because it is more commercially marketable abroad. Placing some of the blame on the Trinidad Tourist Board, Manning (1983b, p. 13) said Trinidad Carnival "has thus become less a popular festival and more a stage spectacle, media event, and tourist attraction."

Music

Popular music in the Caribbean always has had an uphill climb, battling for a place with United States and European sounds. Radio stations, for years, played predominantly foreign music of the Billboard

Top 20 or 40 variety. Since the 1970s, some stations in the British and Dutch islands have instituted policies requiring a percentage of broadcast time for Caribbean music.

Whether because of this policy, or on its own merit, Caribbean music has caught on in the Caribbean, North America, and Europe, making the region an exporter of music. Among exportable popular music are *zouk* of Martinique and Guadeloupe and reggae of Jamaica.

Since the mid-1980s, *zouk*, a type of music relying on rhythm, participatory singing, and dance, has been number one on French Antilles radio charts; it has also sold better in the rest of the Caribbean, Africa, and Europe than any previous Creole music. Guilbault (1987b, p. 9) has written an interesting analysis of *zouk*, calling it carnival music and "music of freedom." She said the music, associated with the Kassav Group, is closely correlated with young people who are unemployed. In five years, the Kassav produced twenty *zouk* albums, several of which became gold platers. Others who have written on French Antilles music are Desroches (1985), on traditional Martiniquan music, and Renard (1981), on popular music of Creole Caribbean. Jallier and Lossen (1985) did an overview of Antillean music in their book, providing lyrics, interviews, and illustrations. The work dealt with the origins and outside influences upon the music, Antillean songs, and contemporary music. Guilbault, who has become one of the most prolific writers on music of Creole Caribbean, has also contributed a monograph on twenty-two musical instruments she identified on St. Lucia (Guilbault, 1983.)

Reggae is probably the best-known Caribbean music worldwide. Numerous writers have described its lyrics and musicians, and its roots in Rastafarianism. Among books are those by Kallyndyr and Dalrymple (1973), Davis and Simon (1977), considered the most useful analysis, Burnett (1982), and White (1983), a biography of the first reggae superstar, Bob Marley. Some periodicals have featured reggae music in articles; among a few of these are *Rolling Stone* (Thomas 1976; McCormack 1976; Cromelin 1975; Crowe 1977; Goodwin 1975), *Village Voice* (Carr 1975; Cooper 1980; Fergusson 1982); *Black Echoes* (Griffith 1976, 1978), *Melody Maker* (Coleman 1976; Goodman 1979; Williams 1972), and *Time* (1976), to name a few.

Reggae, which evolved over fifteen years with African, Jamaican, and United States influences, is one of the very few distinctly Jamaican music forms. It developed when Jamaican artists combined rhythm and blues with their own mento to form the bluebeat, which was followed by the ska, then rock-steady, and finally, reggae. The music uses themes of ghetto protest, religious/philosophical expressions of Rastafarianism, black awareness, and freedom from oppression. Winders (1983, p. 67) labelled it Jamaican music produced in Jamaica, the music of the slums of Trenchtown, and Jamaica's major export, rivalling bauxite.

Hebdige (1977, p. 430), in a short, but worthwhile, history of reggae, discussed its use by Manley and other politicians, as well as its chances of survival. He believed reggae's form guaranteed autonomy and resistance to outside influences. Hebdige's description of reggae is worth quoting: "transmogrified American 'soul' music, with an overlay of salvaged African rhythms, and an undercurrent of pure Jamaican rebellion." Bilby (1977, p. 17), relating the United States' reluctant interest in reggae, said a breakthrough was 1977, when CBS Records bought Jamaica's Federal Records, and with other foreign record companies, promoted reggae as a way of life. He classified reggae as popular music, with also urban folk music (Bilby 1977: 18).

Cuthbert (1985, p. 385) provided one of the few empirical studies on Caribbean music and its audience. Surveying 300 Jamaican youth, she found that reggae was the favorite of only lower socio-economic youth; that of the favorite singers of Jamaican youth, six were foreign and four, local (three of whom were reggae), and that upper class teenagers preferred the imported music.

Because it calls attention to parts of Jamaica the government is not proud of, reggae is banned from radio until after midnight and is not represented as a West Indian art form at the Caribbean Festival of the Arts. Jamaicans hear reggae at dance halls, where they tape the music; they also purchase records from independent recording studios which also own record shops. Thus, as Rastafarian psychologist Leachim Semaj said, reggae is part of Jamaican popular culture, not the national culture. Other sources on reggae and/or Rastafarianism are de Albuquerque (1979), Huey (1981), Gritter (1980), Farrell (1976), Reckford (1982), Spencer (1975, 1977), and Steffens (1981).

On the broader topic of Jamaican music, Clarke (1980) wrote of its evolution in his book, *Jah Music*, and Garth White did two long articles, one tracing traditional music and its influence upon popular music (1982), the other showing the merger of the two (1984). O'Gorman (1972) wrote on studying Jamaican music, and a bibliography on Bob Marley was made available through the National Library of Jamaica.

A music form that has come under closer academic scrutiny is calypso, perhaps because of its political content and use. From at least 1898, when Calypsonian Richard Coeur de Leon attacked the British for wanting to abolish the Port of Spain City Council, the political content was present. Since then, politicians, among them Maurice Bishop, Albert Gomes, and Eric Williams, recognized the clout of calypso. In recent years, calypso has been the subject of a 1986 seminar held in Trinidad (see Marshall 1986), a controversial debate about its origins (one writer claiming Barbados in 1627), and numerous articles.

At least one calypsonian, "The Mighty Sparrow," has put down some of his memoirs in a 1986 Inprint booklet, for the occasion of his fiftieth birthday. Although a beginning, with reminisces by other calypsonians, his teachers, and his wife, the booklet is poorly organized and lacks substantial content (see Sealy 1986 review). Perhaps more interesting is an article that resulted when the Association for Caribbean Studies, at its 1985 meeting, invited "The Mighty Sparrow" (Slinger Francisco) and "Lord Kitchener" (Aldwin Roberts) to talk about calypso. Their insights on the meaning, purpose, and competition of calypso are presented in the *Journal of Caribbean Studies* (Dathorne 1985-86). Earlier, another calypso singer, Raymond Quevedo ("Atilla the Hun") did an excellent study of calypso up to 1951 (Quevedo 1983), in which he discussed the music's development, his role, and the lyrics, many of which are included, along with the musical score and photographs. Lashley (1982) wrote his doctoral dissertation at Howard University on the genre, and the June 1985 issue of *Caribbean Quarterly* carried the theme of "Carnival Calypso and the Music of Confrontation."

Among periodical literature, works by Lewis, McLean, Manning, Elder, and Austin stand out. Lewis (1981) concentrated on the music of "The Mighty Shadow" (Winston Bailey), analyzing the lyrics, citing many verses, and meshing them all with what Bailey said in an interview. Lewis went further to describe calypso's occasional tendency towards violence, cruelty, and belligerence, to briefly trace the music's genesis, and to offer the following definition:

One of the Caribbean's most outstanding art forms is the Trinidadian calypso. More than a "spontaneous typical West Indian song," the calypso has long since metamorphosed from early spontaneous outpourings to a sophisticated and profound socio-political and cultural medium of expression. Not only has the calypso matured in terms of its lyrical content, but also in terms of its ability to incorporate other musical sounds into its own, e.g., the creativity demonstrated in the attempt to combine North American Soul and Disco music with the calypso. These attempts are evident in Lord Beckette's (Alston Cyrus Beckette) Disco-calypsoes and the popular Soca (soul and calypso) music originated by Lord Shortie (Garfield Blackmah) (Lewis 1981: 20).

Looking at the use and impact of calypso before and during Maurice Bishop's Revolution on Grenada, McLean (1986) studied the work of Cecil Belfon ("Flying Turkey"). She said that in 1976, Belfon talked to Bishop about a breakaway calypso tent, called "We Tent," which opened a year later and was useful to Bishop's New Jewel Movement, otherwise shut out of formal media. After the 1979 Revolution, Belfon, with other progressive calypsonians, pushed the Revolution's idealism, education, and political aims, in the process, "bridging the gap between the content of the song and the Party's policies" (McLean 1986: 92).

McLean (1986, p. 87) also provided a compact list of uses for calypso as follows 1. vehicle of social and political protest, 2. device to analyze male/female relationships, 3. medium of information and agitation, 4. means of highlighting a country's economic dilemma and internal contradictions, 5. exercise in institutional abuse, 6. avenue to explore imbalances between the haves and the have—nots, and, 7. part of the cultural heritage of the region.

Calypso and politics in Trinidad and Tobago, St. Vincent, and Barbados is the subject of Manning's article. Showing how smaller islands now claim some of the best calypsonians, Manning said these men are also among the region's most volatile politically. He described the devastating effects Becket's "Horn for Them" had upon the bid of the ruling party in St. Vincent's 1984 election, and "The Mighty Gabby's" role as a thorn in the side of Barbados prime minister, the late Tom Adams. Gabby's songs, most of which were banned from radio, included the popular "Boots," against Barbados militarization; "Mr.T," about stealing votes; "Jack," against an official who wanted to keep Barbadians off the beaches, and "Culture," on U.S. cultural invasion of the Caribbean. Richards (1986), who portrayed Gabby in some detail, attributed revolutionary and radical qualities to his music. Hylton (1975) also looked at the political role of calypso, while Roberts (1972) discussed calypso as one aspect of black music.

One of the first Caribbean academicians to carry out indepth research on calypso was Jacob Elder, who wrote about male—female relationships in the music (1968), and later, a book on calypso's morphology (1973). Elder, in a content analysis of 107 calypsos, reported that there were more aggressive than non-aggressive songs, that the female theme predominated over that of the male, and that aggressiveness towards males in songs decreased over the years. In his psychoanalysis of calypso, the author probed the male's hostility to the mother in West Indian society (Elder 1968).

Critiquing Elder's work, Austin (1976, p. 76) stated that the aggression in calypso towards the mother cannot be inferred from aggressive remarks made about women. In a rambling essay which has much more to say about male—female relationships than it does about calypso, Austin said calypsonians sing about sex because their lower class audiences traditionally appreciated boasting of sexual feats. Modern audiences, according to Austin, are better educated, the result being more varied lyrics and less focus on negative aspects of women (Austin 1976: 80-81).

In a different type of study, Malm and Wallis (1985) compared Trinidad's calypso with Sri Lanka's *baila*.

Another Carnival derivative, steel band, was featured in a book by Bartholomew (1980) and a slide/tape program by Aho (1989). Many types of Caribbean music (ska, calypso, reggae, etc.) made up a book by Hebdige (1987). Hebdige traced the roots of the music, described its style and the sense of cultural identity that developed alongside it, and showed how Caribbean music left impacts in the U.S. and England. Pearse (1978-79) also scanned the spectrum of Caribbean music and related it to popular culture, while Thompson (1980) analyzed music content of Puerto Rican newspapers during the Spanish colonial period. Jenkins and Jenkins (1982) and Hadel (1973) wrote about Garifuna and Carib music, respectively, in Belize.

Film

The Caribbean country with established and competitive film is Cuba, where international film festivals and training schemes are regularly offered.

Cuban film is very well documented in the regularly—published, quality periodical, *Cine Cubano*, and many books and articles. Indices to *Cine Cubano* and filmographies have been compiled by Douglas (1980), Esquieu (1979), and García Mesa (1977). The famous documentary director, Santiago Alvarez (1975), wrote a book on cinema and the Revolution, and Fanshel (1982) compiled seven interviews with famous directors and critiques of twenty films into a volume. Other books were written by Fornet (1982) and Chanan (1985).

Julianne Burton (1977, 1978) has written profusely on Cuban popular culture and film; usually her work takes the form of interviews. Her interview with Manuel Octavio Gomez on popular culture appears in *Jump/Cut* (1979), while valuable interviews with Julio García Espinosa on theory and practice of film and popular culture were published in *Studies in Latin American Popular Culture* (1981) and *Quarterly Review of Film Studies* (1982). Besides these, other periodicals that have had occasional articles are *Afterimage, Film Quarterly, Cineaste, Pensamiento Crítico, Arte, Granma Weekly Review,* and *Sight and Sound* (see Lent 1981, forthcoming).

Literature on film in the rest of the Caribbean is made up of scattered articles, discussing local films in the few producing countries and audiences and locations for foreign film. Concerning the Netherlands Antilles, *De West-Indische Gids* (1948) provided statistics on cinema viewing; van Gorkom (1959) and Swindels (1977) wrote on film in Suriname. Commonwealth Caribbean film is served with occasional articles, one of the oldest being Sellers (1951), as well as reviews of the few locally-produced films, such as "The Harder They Come" and "Countryman," both from Jamaica. Sierra (1980) wrote a thirty-page piece on Dominican Republic film. *Variety*, especially in its special editions or sections on Latin America, carries up-to-date, journalistic accounts of film businesses in the islands.

Sports

Sports perform a very important role in Caribbean popular culture, cricket, soccer, and baseball traditionally being the most popular. However, the Mandles (1988) showed that, in the 1980s, basketball has increased in popularity, partly because of the televised National Basketball Association games received from the U.S. via satellite overspill and/or cable. Using participant—observation, they studied many basketball players in Trinidad and Tobago, where Jay, a referee, gave clinics.

Cricket's significance in the Commonwealth Caribbean is attested to by the festivals built around it. Manning (1981) examined the festival in Bermuda, which, he said, is next to Christmas as the major celebration. After discussing the festival's social history, carnivalesque character, and the ancillary activity of gambling, Manning took the reader on a tour of a cricket festival. He proposed that the festivals symbolically depicted a "reflexive, assertive sense of black culture and a stark awareness of black economic dependency on whites." In an earlier article, Manning (1973) did the same type of analysis of cricket clubs of black Bermudians, reporting they had evolved into major centers of sport, entertainment, and sociability. St. Pierre (1973) also wrote about West Indian cricket devoting considerable attention to the racial composition of the teams, and C.L.R. James (1963), the noted historian, teacher, and journalist, analyzed the game in his autobiography.

In Cuba and the Dominican Republic, baseball is favored. The history of Cuban baseball has been well studied in books by Hernandez (1969), Enriquez (1968), and Capteillo (1971). Pickering (1978) treated Cuban baseball as part of his volume on sports in Communist countries. A provocative book by Krich (1989) discusses baseball in Latin America.

Fimrite (1977) provided empirical evidence about baseball's popularity among Cubans. He content analyzed *Semanario Deportivo LPV*, the leading Cuban sports periodical, from 1969 through 1972. He said the periodical usually devoted seven of its thirty-six pages to baseball; thirty of 127 covers featured this sport. Wagner (1982 and 1988) compared baseball in Cuba and Nicaragua, two Latin American countries in the throes of revolution. He provided an overview of the sport's development, role, and success in Cuba. Fidel's philosophy concerning this U.S. import is that sport is the right of the people, integrated into the Revolution. According to Wagner, baseball came to Cuba in 1864, and when the popular classes assumed power in 1959, the sport came with them.

Comic Art

Although cartoonists exist throughout the Caribbean, only in Cuba are cartoons and comics an established popular art. The Cubans sponsor international humor festivals at least yearly and publish humor magazines. *Dedeté*, published as a weekly supplement of *Juventud Rebelde*, consists mainly of the work of Cuba's famous gag and political cartoonists.

Reporting regularly upon Cuban cartoonists and other graphic artists are *Granma Weekly Review*, the English-language overseas edition of the national daily,[1] *CEMEDIM*, and *UPEC*, the latter two published for journalists in Havana.

In the Commonwealth Caribbean, the literature on comic art is very sparse, thus, journalistic treatments when they appear, such as those in *Caribbean Contact* (February 1975, p. 4; April 1975, p. 4), become very useful. Anthologies of political cartoons have been published in at least Trinidad and Guyana. Hitchins (1959) collected political cartoons that appeared in the *Trinidad Guardian* and *Sunday Guardian*, 1954-59, while the *Mirror*, opposition newspaper of the Jagans in Guyana, pulled together a number of its cartoons that attacked the Forbes Burnham government. Tarter (1985), in his University of Washington thesis on Haiti, devoted some attention to cartoons.

Haiti's revolutionary wall murals (although not humorous, they are part of graphic popular culture) were being studied by David Nicholls and Pablo Butcher in 1988-89.

Conclusion

Other aspects of Caribbean popular culture have been dealt with, such as satire and literature (Crowley 1977), funeral wakes and their music in St. Lucia (Guilbault 1987a), nicknames and license plates as identification and cultural placement (Manning 1974), and the internationally—known posters (Goldman 1984) and public graphics of Cuba (Kunzle 1975). Popular drama has been studied in journals on theater in Cuba and literature in the West Indies, in a larger manuscript by Ford—Smith (1980), and many articles, including those that made up a special issue of *Carib* (1986) on "Caribbean Theatre." That issue had articles on theater in Jamaica and the French West Indies. The latter area is covered in works by Jeanne (1980) and Zobdar-Quitman (1981). Cornevin (1973) wrote on Haitian theater.

Much remains to be accomplished. On a general level, there is a need for a center that would integrate into a whole aspects of popular culture, preserve its artifacts, and record its traditions through oral histories with pioneering artists. This work should not be isolated to one island or island group, but rather, should include the entire region. A university curriculum on popular culture, eventually leading to a diploma or degree, would help legitimize the field of study.

Specifically, some popular culture genres have received less attention than others. More study of topics such as comic art, steel band, or various popular sports is called for, as well as the cultural policies of various governments.

Works Cited

Abrahams, Roger. 1970. "Patterns of Performance in the British West Indies." In *Afro-American Anthropology: Contemporary Perspectives*, edited by Norman Whitten, Jr. and John Szwed, pp. 163-179. New York: The Free Press.

———. and Richard Bauman. 1978. "Ranges of Festival Behaviour." In *The Reversible World: Symbolic Inversion in Art and Society*, edited by Barbara Babcock, pp. 193-208. Ithaca, N.Y.: Cornell University Press.

Aho, William. 1989. *Steelband Music in Trinidad and Tobago.* Providence, R.I.: Author. 32 minutes.

Alvarez, Santiago et al. 1975.*Cine y Revolución en Cuba.* Barcelona: Editorial Fontamara.

Austin, Roy. 1976. "Understanding Calypso Content: A Critique and an Alternative." *Caribbean Quarterly.* June-September, pp. 74-89.

Bartholomew, John. 1980. *The Steel Pan.* London: Oxford University Press.

Bilby, Kenneth. 1977. "The Impact of Reggae in the United States." *Popular Music in Society.* 5:5, pp. 17-22.

Boyke, Roy, ed. 1973. *Trinidad Carnival: The Greatest Spectacle on Earth.* Port of Spain, Trinidad: Kepy Caribbean Publication.

Briceño, Jaime. 1981. "Carnival in Northern Belize." *Belizean Studies.* May.

Brown, Aggrey and Roderick Sanatan. 1987. *Talking with Whom? A Report on the State of the Media in the Caribbean.* Mona, Jamaica: CARIMAC, University of the West Indies.

Burnett, Michael. 1982. *Jamaican Music.* London: Oxford University Press.

Burton, Julianne. 1977. "Film: Revolutionary Cuban Cinema." *Handbook for Latin American Studies.* No. 39, pp. 425-434.

———. 1978. "The Camera as 'Gun': Two Decades of Culture and Resistance in Latin America." *Latin American Perspectives.* Winter, pp. 49-76.

———. 1979. "Popular Culture and Perpetual Quest: An Interview with Manual Octavio Gomez."*Jump/Cut.* May, pp. 17-20.

———. 1981. "Folk Music, Circuses, Variety Shows and Other Endangered Species: A Conversation with Julio García Espinosa on the Preservation of Popular Culture in Cuba." *Studies in Latin American Popular Culture.* 1, pp. 216-223.

———. 1982. "Theory and Practice of Film and Popular Culture in Cuba: A Conversation with Julio García Espinosa." *Quarterly Review of Film Studies.* Fall, pp. 341—351.

Capteillo, Enrique. 1971. "103 Años de Lucha, 105 Años de Beisbol." *Semanario Deportivo LPV.* 30 November, pp. 14—17.

Carib. 1986. "Caribbean Theatre." No. 4, pp. 1—78.

Caribbean Contact. February 1975, "Cartoon—As an Instrument for Development," p. 16.

———. April 1975, "Cartoonists at Work," p. 4.

———. 1987. "Literature and Theatre in C'bean." June, p. 7.

Carnival: St. Vincent and the Grenadines. n.d. Kingstown, St. Vincent: NMM Associates.

Carr, Patrick. 1975. "Bob Marley Is the Jagger of Reggae." *Village Voice*, 30 June.

Cartoons from the Mirror. 1974. Georgetown, Guyana: New Guyana Co., Ltd. October.

Chanan, Michael. 1985. *The Cuban Image: Cinema and Cultural Politics in Cuba.* Bloomington: Indiana University Press.

Clarke, Sebastian. 1980. *Jah Music—The Evolution of Popular Jamaican Song.* London: Heinemann.

Cohen, Abner. 1980. "Drama and Politics in the Development of a London Carnival." *Man* (n.s.). 15, pp. 65—87.

_____ 1982. "A Polyethnic London Carnival as a Contested Cultural Performance." *Ethnic and Racial Studies*, 5:1, pp. 23-41.

Coleman, Ray. 1976. "Root Strong in Funky Kingston." *Melody Maker*, 12 June.

Cooper, Carol. 1980. "Tuff Gong: Bob Marley's Unsung Story." *Village Voice*, 10 September.

Cornevin, Robert. 1973. *Le Theatre Haitien des Origenes a Nos Jours*, Montreal.

Cromelin, Richard. 1975. "An Herbal Meditation with Bob Marley." *Rolling Stone*, 11 September.

Crowe, Cameron. 1977. "Bob Marley: The Shooting of a Wailer." *Rolling Stone*, 11 January.

Crowley, Daniel. 1955. "Festivals of the Calendar in St. Lucia." *Caribbean Quarterly*, 4, pp. 99—121.

_____ 1956. "The Traditional Masques of Carnival." *Caribbean Quarterly*, 4, pp. 194—223.

_____ ed. 1977. *African Folklores in the New World*, Austin: University of Texas Press.

Cuthbert, Marlene. 1985. "Cultural Autonomy and Popular Music: A Survey of Jamaican Youth." *Communication Research*, July, pp. 381—393.

_____ and Michael Pidgeon, eds. 1981. *Language and Communication in the Caribbean*, Bridgetown, Barbados: Cedar Press.

Dathorne, O.R. 1985—86. "A Kind of Picong: A Dialogue Between Lord Kitchener and the Mighty Sparrow." *Journal of Caribbean Studies*, Fall/Spring, pp. 57—68.

Davis, Stephen. 1975. "Reggae—Jamaica's Inside-Out Rock and Roll." *New York Times*, 30 November.

_____ and Peter Simon. 1977. *Reggae Bloodlines: In Search of the Music and Culture of Jamaica*, Garden City, N.Y.: Anchor.

de Albuquerque, Klaus. 1979. "The Future of the Rastafarian Movement." *Caribbean Review*, 8:4, pp. 22—25, 44—46.

Desroches, Monique. 1985. *La Musique Traditionelle de la Martinique*, Montreal: Centre de Recherches Caraïbes de l'Université de Montreal.

Devoss, David. 1977. "The Reggae Message." *Human Behavior*, January, pp. 64-69.

Douglas, Maria E. 1980. *Filmografia del Cine Cubano, 1959—Julio, 1980*, Havana: Cinematica de Cuba, Seccion de Cine Cubano, October.

Elder, Jacob D. 1968. "The Male—Female Conflict in Calypso." *Caribbean Quarterly*, September, pp. 23-41.

_____ 1973. *The Calypso and Its Morphology*, Port of Spain, Trinidad: National Cultural Council.

Enriquez, Celso. 1968. *Sports in Pre—Hispanic America*, Mexico, D.F.: Litografica Machado, S.A.

Esquieu, Gloria. 1979. *Indice de la Revista Cine Cubano, 1960—1974*, Havana: Bibliateca Nacional José Martí.

Fanshel, Susan. 1982. *A Decade of Cuban Documentary Film, 1972-1982*. New York: Young Filmmakers Inc.

Farrell, Barry. 1976. "Bob Marley—The Visionary as Sex Symbol." *Chic*. November.

Fergusson, Isaac. 1982. " 'So Much Things To Say'—The Journey of Bob Marley." *Village Voice*, 18 May.

Fimrite, Ron. 1977. "In Cuba, It's Viva El Grand Old Game." *Sports Illustrated*, 6 June, pp. 68—80.

Ford-Smith, Honor. 1980. *SISTREN: Women's Theatre and Community Education*, Kingston: Jamaica School of Drama, Cultural Training Centre. Unpublished manuscript.

Fornet, Ambrosio. 1982. *Cine, Literatura, Sociedad*, Havana: Editorial Letras Cubanas.

García Mesa, Héctor. 1977. *Catálogo General del Cine Cubano, 1897—1975*. 2 vols.

Goldman, Shifra M. 1984. "Painters into Poster Makers: Two Views Concerning the History, Aesthetics and Ideology of the Cuban Poster Movement." *Studies in Latin American Popular Culture*, 3, pp. 162—173.

Goldman, Vivien. 1979. "Bob Marley in His Own Backyard." *Melody Maker*, 11 August.

Goodwin, Michael. 1975. "Marley, the Maytals and the Reggae Armageddon." *Rolling Stone*, 11 September.

Griffith, Pat. 1976. "Shanker in Action." *Black Echoes*, August.

———. 1978. "The Drug in Reggae." *Black Echoes*, January.

Gritter, Headley. 1980. "The Magic of Bob Marley." *Record Review*. April.

Guilbault, Jocelyne. 1983. *Instruments Musicaux a Sainte-Lucie*, Paris: Agence de Coopération Culturelle et Technique.

———. 1987a. "Fitness and Flexibility: Funeral Wakes in St. Lucia, West Indies." *Ethnomusicology*, 3:2, pp. 273—299.

———. 1987b. "When the Third World Music Becomes a World—Wide Hit." Paper read at American Musicological Society, 26 September, Ottawa, Canada. Mimeographed.

———. Forthcoming. "La Musique Créole: Dynamisme et Authenticite." *Francophonie*.

Hadel, Richard E. 1973. "Carib Dance Music and Dance." *Belizean Studies*. November.

Hebdige, Dick. 1977. "Reggae, Rastas and Rudies." In *Mass Communication and Society*, edited by James Curran et al., pp. 426—439, London: Edward Arnold.

———. 1987. *Cut N' Mix: Culture, Identity and Caribbean Music*, New York: Routledge.

Hernandez, Luis. 1969. "Un Siglo de Beisbol en Cuba." *Semanario Deportivo LPV*, 2 December, pp. 8—9.

Hill, Errol. 1972. *The Trinidad Carnival: Mandate for a National Theatre*, Austin: University of Texas Press.

Hitchins, William E. 1959. *J.M. and Other Cartoonists from the Trinidad Guardian*, Port of Spain: Trinidad Publishing Co. Ltd.

Huey, John. 1981. "Hypnotic Sound of Reggae Floats Far From the the Slums of Jamaica." *Wall Street Journal*, 10 August.

Hylton, Patrick. 1975. "The Politics of Caribbean Music." *The Black Scholar*, September, pp. 23—29.

Jallier, Maurice and Yollen Lossen. 1985. *Musique aux Antilles. Mizak bo Kay*, Paris: Editions Caribecnnes.

James, C.L.R. 1963. *Beyond a Boundary*, London: Hutchinson.

Jeanne, Max. 1980. "Sociologie du Theatre Antillais." *CARE*, May.

Jenkins, Carol and Travis Jenkins. 1982. "Garifuna Musical Style and Culture History." *Belizean Studies*, 10: 3/4

Kallyndyr, Rolston and Henderson Dalrymple. 1973. *Reggae: A People's Music*, London: Carib-Arawak Publications.

Krich, John. 1989. *El Beisbol: Travels Through the Pan-American Pastime*, New York: Atlantic Monthly Press.

Kunzle, David. 1975. "Public Graphics in Cuba: A Very Cuban Form of International Art." *Latin American Perspectives*. 2:4, pp. 91 +.

Lashley, Leroy Lennox George. 1982. "An Analysis of the Calypso As a Mass Communication Medium: The Social and Political Uses (Trinidad)." Ph.D. dissertation, Howard University.

Lent, John A. 1977. *Third World Mass Media and Their Search for Modernity*: Cranbury, N.J.: Associated Universities Press.

———— 1981. *Caribbean Mass Communications: A Comprehensive Bibliography*. Waltham, MA.: Crossroads Press.

———— Forthcoming. *Bibliographic Guide to Caribbean Mass Communications*.

Lewis, George H. 1979. "Mass, Popular, Folk, and Elite Cultures: Webs of Significance." *Media Asia*, 6:1, pp. 34—43.

Lewis, Linden. 1981. "The Mighty Shadow: On the Pointlessness of Human Existence." *Caribbean Review*, Fall, pp. 20-23, 49—50.

Malm, Krister and Roger Wallis. 1985. "The *Baila* of Sri Lanka and the Calypso of Trinidad." *Communication Research*, July, pp 277—300.

Mandle, Jay R. and Joan D. Mandle. 1988. "Grassroots Commitment: Dependency and Creativity in Trinidad and Tobago Basketball." Paper read at Caribbean Studies Association, 25 May, Guadeloupe. Mimeographed.

Manning, Frank. 1973. *Black Clubs in Bermuda: Ethnography of a Play World*, Ithaca, N.Y.: Cornell University Press.

———— 1974. "Nicknames and Number Plates in the British West Indies." *Journal of American Folklore*, April—June, pp. 123-132.

———— 1978. "Carnival in Antigua: An Indigenous Festival in a Tourist Economy." *Anthropos*, 73, pp. 191—204.

———— 1981. "Celebrating Cricket: The Symbolic Construction of Caribbean Politics." *American Ethnologist*, pp. 616-632.

———— 1983a. "Carnival in the West Indian Diaspora.*The Round Table*, 286, pp. 186—196.

———— 1983b. "The Carnival Industry." *The Caribbean and West Indies Chronicle*. April—May, pp. 12—13.

———— 1984. "The Performance of Politics: Caribbean Music and the Anthropology of Victor Turner." *Anthropologica*, 26:1.

———— 1986. "Challenging Authority: Calypso and Politics in the Caribbean." In *The Frailty of Authority*, edited by Myron J. Aronoff, pp. 167—179. New Brunswick, N.J.: Transaction Books.

Marshall, Trevor. 1986. "Calypso—A Caribbean Journey." *Caribbean Contact*. February, p. 12.

McCormack, Ed. 1976. "Bob Marley with a Bullet." *Rolling Stone*. 12 August, pp. 37—41.

McLean, Polly. 1986. "Calypso and Revolution in Grenada." *Popular Music and Society*, 10:4, pp. 87—99.

Nettleford, Rex M. 1979. *Cultural Action and Social Change: The Case of Jamaica. An Essay in Caribbean Cultural Identity*, Ottawa: International Development Research Centre.

O'Gorman, Pam. 1972. "An Approach to the Study of Jamaican Popular Music." *Jamaica Journal*, December.

Pearse, Andrew. 1955. "Aspects of Change in Caribbean Folk Music." *Journal of the International Folk Music Council*, 7, pp. 29—36.

———— 1956. "Carnival in Nineteenth Century Trinidad." *Caribbean Quarterly*, 4, pp. 176—193.

———— 1969. "Mitto Sampson on Calypso Legends of the Nineteenth Century." *Caribbean Quarterly*, 15, pp. 2—3.

———— 1978/79. "Music in Caribbean Popular Culture." *Revista Interamericana*, Winter, pp. 629—39.

Pickering, R.J. 1978. "Cuba." In *Sport Under Communism*, edited by James Riordan, pp. 148—149. London: C. Hurst.

Quevedo, Raymond. 1983. *Atilla's Kaiso: A Short History of Trinidad Calypso*, St Augustine, Trinidad: University of the West Indies.

Reckford, V. 1982. "Reggae, Rastafarianism and Cultural Identity." *Jamaica Journal*, 46, pp. 69—79.

Renard, Yves. 1981. "Kadans: Musique Populaire de la Caraïbe Créolophone, Facteur d'Intégration Régionale?" Paper read at Troisième Colloque International des Etudes Créoles, 3—9 May, St. Lucia. Mimeographed.

Richard, Michael. 1986. "Mighty Calypsonian: Controversial Gabby." *Caribbean Contact*, January, p. 12.

Roberts, John S. 1972. *Black Music of Two Worlds*, New York: Praeger.

Rohlehr, Gordon. 1972. "Forty Years of Calypso." *Tapia*, 2, pp. 3-16.

Sealy, Clifford. 1986. "Unjust to a Genius." *Caribbean Contact*, May, p. 15.

Sellers, W. 1951. "Film Production in the West Indies." *Colonial Cinema*, December, pp. 91—92.

Sierra, Julio. 1980. *Cine en Santo Domingo*. Santo Domingo: Comite Pro Instituto Nacional de Estudios Cinematograficos.

Soderlund, Walter C. and Stuart H. Surlin, eds. 1985. *Media in Latin America and the Caribbean: Domestic and International Perspectives*, Windsor, Canada: University of Windsor.

Spencer, Neil. 1975. "Me Just Wanna Live, Y'unnerstan?" *New Musical Express*, 19 July.

———— 1977. "Me No Political Man—Inside Bob Marley's UK Hideaway." *New Musical Express*, 23 April.

Steffens, Roger. 1981. "Dreadlocks Forever—The Life and Death of Bob Marley." *Los Angeles Reader*, 22 May.

St. Pierre, Maurice. 1973. "West Indian Cricket: A Sociohistorical Appraisal." *Caribbean Quarterly*. 19, pp. 7—27.

Swindels, J. 1977. "Filmkunst." In *Cultureel Mosaïek van Suriname. Bijdrage tot Onderling Begrip*, edited by Albert Helman, pp. 407—411. De Walburg Pers Zutphen, C.F.J. Schriks.

Tarter, William Vernon. 1985. " 'Many Hands—Load Not Heavy'; A Study of Participatory Communication in Rural Haiti." Master's Thesis, University of Washington.

Taylor, Patrick. 1989. *The Narrative of Liberation: Perspectives on Afro-Caribbean Literature, Popular Culture, and Politics*, Ithaca, N.Y.: Cornell University Press.

Thomas, Michael. 1976. "The Rastas Are Coming! The Rastas Are Coming!" *Rolling Stone*, 12 August, p. 34.

Thompson, Annie. 1980. "Puerto Rican Newspapers and Journals of the Spanish Colonial Period as Source Materials for Musicological Research: An Analysis of Their Musical Content." Ph.D. dissertation, Florida State University.

Time. 1976. "Singing Them a Message." 22 March, pp. 83—84.

Van Gorkom, J.A.J. 1959. "Filmkunst in Suriname." *Wikor*, 7:3, pp. 104—106.

Wagner, Eric. 1982. "Sport After Revolution: A Comparative Study of Cuba and Nicaragua." *Studies in Latin American Popular Culture*, 1, pp. 65—73.

_____ 1984. "Baseball in Cuba." *Journal of Popular Culture*, Summer, pp. 113—120.

_____ 1988. "Sport in Revolutionary Societies: Cuba and Nicaragua." In *Sport and Society in Latin America*. edited by Joseph L. Arbena, Westport, Ct: Greenwood Press.

Warner, Keith Q. 1982. *Kaiso! The Trinidad Calypso: A Study of the Calypso As Oral Literature*. Washington, D.C.: Three Continents Press.

White, Garth. 1982. "Traditional Musical Practice in Jamaica and its Influence on The Birth of Modern Jamaican Popular Music." *ACIJ Newsletter*, No. 7, March, pp. 41—67.

_____ 1984. "The Development of Jamaican Popular Music—Pt. 2. Urbanisation of the Folk: The Merger of the Traditional and the Popular in Jamaican Music." *ACIJ Research Review*. No. 1, pp. 47—80.

White, Timothy. 1983. *Catch a Fire: The Life of Bob Marley*.

Williams, Richard. 1972. "The Facts of Reggae." *Melody Maker*, 19 February.

Wilson, Peter. 1973. *Crab Antics: The Social Anthropology of English Speaking Negroes in the Societies of the Caribbean*, New Haven: Yale University Press.

Winders, James A. 1983. "Reggae, Rastafarians and Revolution: Rock Music in the Third World. *Journal of Popular Culture*, Summer, pp. 61—73.

Zobdar—Quitman, Soniar. 1981. *Culture et Politique en Guadeloupe et Martinique*, Paris: Editions Alizes—Karthala.

Chapter Two
Overseas Caribbean Carnivals
The Art and Politics of a Transnational Celebration

Frank E. Manning

While Third World countries are well known as importers of metropolitan popular culture, the reverse process—the export of cultural products and performances from the Third World—has evoked less discussion. Nowhere is this latter process better illustrated than in the Caribbean, where the export of popular entertainment has become a significant multinational industry. The dynamics of this industry constitute an important social, political, and economic link between the Caribbean and the metropolis, reversing the conventional geography of the center-periphery relationship and exemplifying, somewhat ironically, McLuhan's prophecy of a cultural global village.

The export of Caribbean entertainment is inseparable from one of the most striking developments in international popular culture in the past quarter century: the emergence of West Indian-style carnivals in several major North American and European cities which have hosted the latest episodes of the Caribbean diaspora. The phenomenon originated in New York in the 1920s and was revived there in 1965, the same year that a similar carnival began in London. Toronto and Montreal followed in 1967, the year of the Canadian centennial. The appeal and potential of these overseas carnivals became more apparent in the 1970s and 1980s. In the US, the list of sponsoring cities grew to include Boston, Hartford, Miami, Washington, Detroit, and Los Angeles. In Canada, carnivals emerged in Hamilton, Winnipeg, and Edmonton.[1] Collectively these carnivals fill the summer calendar and rank high among the public performances that have injected new energy and interest into urban life (Kirschenblatt-Gimblett 1983).

As a symbolic and institutional form, carnival lies at the core of a "transnational sociocultural system," a phrase used by Sutton to describe the consequences of the massive immigration of Caribbean peoples to the metropolitan world, their distinctive proclivity for propagating their cultural tastes, and their determination to maintain close contact with their homelands (Sutton 1987: 15-30). This transnational system exhibits

The Hon. Lily Munro, Ontario Minister of Citizenship and Culture, leads the way down University Avenue on Carnival day.

a broad range of unity and diversity, a balance exemplified by the general sameness of the overseas carnivals as well as their many specific differences. The overseas carnivals thus lend themselves to the type of comparative study that immigration scholars like Segal have recently advocated, but which has yet to be undertaken in any comprehensive manner (Segal 1987: 57).

Symbolism and Strategy

Each overseas carnival is meant to be, after a fashion, a symbolic reconstruction of the famous Trinidad Carnival, which is acknowledged both as the source and most spectacular manifestation of the carnival form in the Caribbean (Hill and Abramson 1979). Trinidadian performance items are therefore showcased; local Trinidadians tend to dominate the organization; and Trinidadian artists, local and imported, have the most prominent roles. But other West Indians, particularly those from the eastern Caribbean, are enthusiastic supporters and participants, partly because their home countries have also recently developed localized modifications of Trinidad's famous carnival. Haitians, another immigrant group conversant with carnival, are also noticeably attracted to the overseas carnivals in cities where they are numerous like Montreal, New York, Boston, and Miami. Even Jamaicans, who do not have a carnival tradition and whose entertainment style is significantly different from that of the eastern Caribbean, tend to be drawn, albeit marginally, into carnival.

The incorporation of different and historically divided Caribbean populations into a single performance system is often problematic. Many of the overseas carnivals have been deeply and acrimoniously factionalized along lines of national origin, to the point of splitting periodically into rival festivals (Manning 1983). Nonetheless, carnival is ideally revered as a symbol and mechanism of pan-Caribbean unity, a demonstration of the fragile but persistent Caribbean belief that "All o' we is one." The "Mighty Sparrow," Trinidad's preeminent calypsonian, expresses this vision in his song "Mas' in Brooklyn." Traditional social divisions are meaningless in New York, Sparrow proposes, because the rest of society "haven't know who is who" and therefore "equalize you;" hence carnival is for "tut mun" (tout le monde, everyone). A carnival enthusiast in Toronto expressed exactly this sentiment, claiming that since Canadians view all West Indians as a single group, they might as well have a common identification with one festival (Manning 1982).

Involvement in the overseas carnivals encourages regular and frequent travel between the metropolitan world and the Caribbean. Each February some fifty thousand carnival enthusiasts—performers, promoters, commentators, costume makers, aficionados and fans of all kinds—return "home" to participate in the Trinidad Carnival. Those journey often describe it as a kind of cultural pilgrimage, an understanding that is endorsed by the Trinidadian anthropologist John Stewart: "Great numbers troop back home annually...for the master celebration. For them, carnival stands as a time of renewal, of self affirmation, which can occur in no other way. To miss carnival is to be diminished" (Stewart 1986: 290-291).

These pilgrims come back to the metropolis as importers of the latest music, fashion, and artistic techniques from the Trinidad Carnival, which they incorporate into their local carnivals months later. This process, which exists on a smaller scale among West Indians from other Caribbean countries, does more than revivify the immigrant's cultural imagination. It also maintains and validates the Caribbean's symbolic domination both of carnival and of the cultural system which it celebrates.

Besides their continuing connections with the Caribbean, the overseas carnivals are connected with each other. A "carnival circuit" has evolved, since the urban carnivals are scheduled to facilitate travel from one to the other. Leading entertainers from the Caribbean now spend most of their working time on this circuit, as the larger carnivals are not single events but "seasons" lasting several weeks. On the non-professional level, organized tours shuttle carnival fans around the circuit by bus or plane. Thousands more travel on their own by car, planning long weekends and summer vacations to coincide with particular carnivals. Some carnival devotees are members of masquerade bands who bring their own costumes and participate as a group. Others make arrangements through family or friends to join bands in the host city. The overseas carnivals also attract an increasing number of enthusiasts from the Caribbean, reversing the winter flow of travel and providing another occasion for renewed contact between the homeland and the metropolis.

Yet Caribbean carnival overseas is more than an international cultural phenomenon. It is also, everywhere it emerges, a consciously political event. Carnival organizers view their enterprise as an occasion for expressing their interests as well as their identity, demonstrating their size, resources, and capacity to mobilize in a metropolitan setting, and building alliances with strategic sectors of the wider community. The nature of this manifold process and the means of pursuing it vary greatly, making each carnival a study in itself. In all cases, however, artistic symbolism and political strategy act upon each other in mutually influential ways. I will consider some of the varieties of this relationship in three very different carnivals—those of Toronto, New York, and London.

Masquerade and Multiculturalism

Legend has it that Trinidad was so named by Columbus because the three peaks which dominated its northern mountain range reminded him of the Holy Trinity. Coincidentally, the Trinidad Carnival is composed of three principal art forms: masquerade, calypso, and steel band. The three forms are found in all overseas carnival, but the relative emphasis on one over the others is politically suggestive.

Masquerade, known simply as "mas' " in Trinidad, is the chief visual attraction of carnival. Each masquerade band depicts a theme, which may be drawn from history, literature, folklore, fantasy, current events, or virtually any domain of popular culture. The king and queen of the band have the most extravagant costumes, often taking months to produce and costing several thousands of dollars in materials alone. Elaborate costumes are also worn by the male and female leaders of each section of the band, and by persons who participate as outstanding "individuals." When the bands go on the road—on foot, not on floats— these star performers are joined by a costumed membership which, in Trinidad, may run as large as four thousand persons, although bands of several hundred persons are more common (Stewart 1986: 307). The popular bands also tend to attract large numbers of non-costumed revelers as they dance their way through the streets.

In Trinidad, the artistic, organizational, and financial leadership of the large masquerade bands—those that produce what is today called "pretty mas' "—has been mostly in the hands of the non-black middle and upper classes: whites and lighter-skinned mulattoes, Chinese, Syrians, Portuguese, and East Indians. The affinity persists after three decades of black political leadership, partly because carnival is now promoted both as a symbol of national unity and as an international tourist attraction. Both promotional claims place a premium on multiracial participation in the most visible area of carnival festivity, and further encourage the trend towards increasingly expensive—and therefore socially exclusive—masquerade productions.

Caribbean immigrants to Canada have been drawn heavily from the social strata associated with masquerading. The flow was greatest in the 1960s and 1970s, when the "points system" favored those with relatively high educational and occupational qualifications (Henry 1987: 215). Non-black West Indians came in disproportionate numbers, as did blacks from middle class backgrounds. Yet, despite their diversity of racial backgrounds, Caribbean immigrants have collectively become "black Canadians" (Henry 1987: 222)—a process encouraged both by the new opportunities available to "visible minorities" and by the absence of a large indigenous black population, particularly in the major cities where most immigrants have settled.[2] Moreover, West Indians have moved at an impressive rate into significant positions in the civil service, the judiciary, the academic world, politics, even business. Although

Adjusting her oversized headpiece, a youthful masquerader celebrates carnival in Toronto.

discrimination undoubtedly exists, the remarkable success of West Indians in Canada is the more striking phenomenon and the one in greater need of sociological analysis.

These and related circumstances are linked to the predominance of masquerade in all of the Caribbean carnival's in Canada. Toronto's Caribana, the largest of these—indeed, the largest ethnic celebration of any kind in Canada—can serve as an example. Caribana is showcased as a major urban event, with the masquerade parade as its centerpiece. The parade begins at Queen's Park, seat of the Ontario legislature. From there it proceeds down University Avenue, a wide, tree-lined boulevard flanked by foreign consular offices, world-class hospitals, international banks, luxury hotels, and corporate headquarters. After six hours or so in this environment, the bands disperse in an area partially enclosed by the Roy Thomson Hall, a fashionable performing arts theater, and a resplendent new convention center-hotel complex. In the near background are two other symbols of urban prestige—the CN Tower and, beside it, the SkyDome. The Caribana parade route is thus a symbolic itinerary through the corridors of wealth and power, a feature that it shares with other Canadian carnivals but that distinguishes it radically from most US and British carnivals, that are held in ghettoized residential neighborhoods.

Caribana's setting and style enhance its value as a tourist attraction. The parade itself draws a half million people onto University Avenue, and the festival generates an estimated $40 million over a period of two weeks. While most of the profit goes to the large hotels and other established, non-Caribbean businesses, West Indians benefit indirectly in the form of publicity and political patronage. Caribana receives massive coverage in the mainstream press, and now has the *Toronto Star*—the largest (in bulk) newspaper in the city—as one of its sponsors. Since 1984 the masquerade parade has been televised live by the Canadian Broadcasting Corporation (CBC), Canada's national network. This coverage has steadily expanded and now includes programs before and after Caribana. Television exposure has further given the masquerade bands the incentive of reaching a much larger audience, increasing their attractiveness to commercial sponsors. There is again a striking contrast here with the Caribbean carnivals in the U.S., which receive little publicity in the mainstream media and fail generally to reach audiences beyond the black community.

Predictably, an event of this type draws the attention of politicians. Since 1983 the masquerade parade has been officially opened by the mayor and one or more provincial cabinet ministers. In 1988, the cast of political dignitaries included a federal cabinet minister. In Canadian fashion, these politicians come with massive patronage resources in the form of grants for the organizing committee. They are also direct sponsors. In 1988 and 1989, for example, the first two masquerade bands were respectively produced by federal and provincial ministries, which paid for the services of West Indian designers, choreographers, and musical units. Not to be upstaged, Ontario's two opposition parties also sponsor masquerade bands and make sure that their leading politicians are prominently involved.

As Caribana grows and gains increasing publicity, it also attracts non-Caribbean participation. In the past few years, there have been masquerade bands made up of black Nova Scotian, Uruguayan, and Ghanian community groups. And in the early and middle 1980s, the parade was graced by a steel band made up of middle-aged Mormon women! Tutored by a Trinidadian musician, the women began as the "LDS (Latter-Day Saints) Steel Band," changing their name later to the more conventional "Sounds of Steel."

But the most interesting new band, which has participated since 1985, is a group of white Canadians known as "Island to Island." A bohemian colony of sorts that live on one of the small islands in the Toronto Harbor and produce protest theater, the group apprenticed themselves to a Trinidadian costume designer in Toronto and developed a connection with The Bamboo Club, a nightclub specializing in Caribbean entertainment. They also started going to the Trinidad Carnival to play mas' with Peter Minshall, the avant-garde, white bandleader who has combined theatrical innovation and sophisticated political criticism in ways that have attracted international acclaim. "Island to Island's" recent productions in Toronto, which clearly bear the stamp of Minshall's influence, include masquerade bands such as "The Late Great Lakes," which depicted the gradual pollution of Lake Ontario, and "Stone Wars Apocalypso," a satire proposing that Ronald Reagan's millenarian program for control of space would bring back the stone age. The latter band included Minshall's prize-winning costume, "The Merry Monarch of Death," which was flown in from Trinidad (Jackson 1987).

Political support for this sort of spectacle goes well beyond traditional forms of ethnic patronage. Caribana, chiefly through its elaborate masquerade show, is a highly visible example of multiculturalism, a Canadian social belief that is officially enshrined and politically unassailable, but necessarily problematic. As the basis of government policy, multiculturalism entails both the active preservation of immigrant cultures and the notion that they are part of a repertory that should be accessible to all Canadians, as spectators, consumers, or participants (Ostry 1978). Caribana's splendid success in filling this demanding role demonstrates that multiculturalism works, confirming Canadian identity and ideology on a much broader scale. Canada needs its Caribbean carnival, giving those who perform it a claim to center stage.

Calypso and Black Ethnicity

The other two artistic components of carnival, calypso music and its most celebrated instrumental expression, the steel band, are oral/aural rather than visual. But the greater distinction is social. While masquerade has been associated especially with the non-black middle and upper classes, calypso and steel band have been, for the most part, the cultural property of the lower black class. Even today calypsonians and steelbandsmen are known as "Bad Johns," hustlers and rogues who use their music to glamorize a lifestyle that is the antithesis of social respectability.

As an industry, calypso has been based in New York since the time of World War I, when the first recordings were made by Lionel "Lanky" Belasco. It was also the time when an initial large influx of West Indian immigrants were settling in Harlem (Hill and Abramson 1979: 77). The industry shifted to Brooklyn in the 1960s, when those who came in another large wave of Caribbean immigrants, blacks especially, found their way to central Brooklyn. Today, the business addresses of the industry's major producers, promoters, distributors, and retailers can be found along a crowded block on Fulton Street between Bedford Avenue and Nostrand Avenue. The core of black Brooklyn is the world capital of calypso.

The Brooklyn Carnival, which began in 1965, is dominated by calypso in much the same way that Toronto's is highlighted by masquerade. The size and cost of costumes can serve as a rough indicator. The largest costumes in Brooklyn are about eight feet round and estimated as having a maximum cost of $800 (Hill, D. 1981: 35). By comparison, the largest costumes in Toronto—those produced by leading bandleaders like Eddie Merchant, Louis Saldenha, Ken Shah, Wallace Alexander, Nip Davis, Russell Charter, Whitfield Belasco, Arnold Hughes, Noel Audain, and several others—may extend the full width of University Avenue's three lanes and carry price tags estimated at ten times higher than their Brooklyn counterparts.

More significantly, Brooklyn's carnival parade is less of a masquerade show than one of many attractions within a sprawling, unfocused street fair. For most carnivalgoers, the real highlight of the festival is the tremendous number of calypso shows and dances that take place before, during, and after the festival—events publicized on huge "cards" glued to the sides of the massive cast-iron garbage bins found on every street corner in Brooklyn. In fact, the calypso season in New York now runs almost year round, as leading international performers maintain residences there and visit regularly for shows, recording sessions, and promotional work. Brooklyn's carnival is the chief epiphany of this activity, the time when it spills aggressively and flamboyantly into the public domain. The climax comes on carnival Saturday, when Rawlston

"Charlie" Charles—identified on his business cards as the "World's Greatest Calypso Producer and Manufacturer"—runs a block party that nearly stops all vehicular traffic outside his Fulton Street record store. Milling through the crowd, one is likely to find a dozen or more calypso celebrities, all maintaining the easy contact and camaraderie with fans that has become the music's endearing hallmark.

As a cultural group, calypso functions to differentiate its West Indian constituency from black America, which is, in central Brooklyn, the surrounding social presence. The means of expressing this ethnic difference—music, electronically amplified—is particularly suited to a black urban environment where "ghetto blasters" are established technological icons. If West Indians are invisible in black America, they are not, especially at carnival time, inaudible.

The issue of ethnic differences is central in black American-West Indian relations, which are characterized by an extraordinary degree of ambivalence. As Nancy Foner (1985) points out, West Indians in New York have benefited greatly from the black American environment in which they have settled. It partially shields them from day-to-day discrimination by whites, provides political representation and institutional support, and gives them opportunities generated by the civil rights movement and subsequent programs. As well, black Americans are a proximate clientele for the many entrepreneurial pursuits—entertainment included—into which West Indians channel their energies. Yet West Indians insist on their separate identity, cherishing both their Caribbean traditions and their stereotype of being harder working than black Americans, more inclined to seek an education, more successful at business and the professions, and, ironically, more acceptable to whites.

Carnival itself has been at times a theater of West Indian-black American conflict. The earlier Carnival in Harlem ended in 1964 when it was violently disrupted by Black Power protestors who viewed West Indian festivity as inimical to their objectives (Nunley 1988: 166). A more interesting episode took place in Brooklyn twenty years later, when Jesse Jackson took his campaign to carnival. A platform was erected in front of the Brooklyn Museum, where the carnival parade disperses, and Jackson spoke there for an hour. During this time all carnival traffic stopped and the sound systems shut down, on order from the police. At the end of the speech, Jackson pleaded with those who were not registered voters to come forward for cards, directing his supporters to open a path to the rostrum.

This incident, which I witnessed in the midst of the crowd, is revealing. As Wiggins (1987) has pointed out, politics intrudes directly into black American community celebrations in the form of speeches, registration drives, and a variety of other practices and performances which tend to reflect the expressive affinity of religion and politics.

Jackson was clearly following this tradition, delivering a moral sermon as much as a political speech and concluding it with an invitation to those unregistered ("unsaved") to correct their condition and leave with a new status and power. But to West Indians, an overwhelming majority of the captive audience, the event was culturally unfamiliar and unwelcome. No one stops carnival in the Caribbean, and a politician who tried would experience a brief career. Moreover, the religious orientations of West Indians tend towards Catholicism and the larger Protestant denominations, rather than the more evangelical churches which hold the allegiance of black Americans. Finally, given estimates of the larger number of undocumented immigrants from the Caribbean in New York, there is the comic irony that a sizable portion of Jackson's audience were not only ineligible to vote, but illegally in the country. There was little evidence of support for Jackson that day, and a great deal of evidence of anger and frustration among a crowd whose music was forcibly muted.

Hence the distinction between West Indians and black Americans, along with its potential for conflict, remains an inescapable fact of life in Brooklyn. Carnival, Jackson's and similar intrusions notwithstanding, is the chief calendrical occasion when West Indians proclaim that they are attached to culture as much as color. The same assertion is made in other Caribbean carnivals in the US, notably those of Boston, Detroit, and Washington, which also take place in residential areas that are ordinarily dominated by American blacks. In all cases, ethnicity enjoys electronic amplification, as the rhythms of the Caribbean are blasted through neighborhoods attuned to the power of sound.

Steel Band and Ritual Violence

The third carnival art form, the steel band, was "invented" a half century ago in Trinidad's urban shantytowns when black street gangs realized that they could make a new kind of musical drum from 55-gallon oil barrels (Hill, E. 1972: 47-48). This unlikely, almost mythical beginning shaped the ambiguous social history of the steel band. On the one hand, the steel band has been an instrument—in the double sense—of violent conflict. Developed in the context of slum neighborhood rivalries, the early bands fought both with each other and with the police who were empowered to keep them off the road. Inheriting a strain of violence in the carnival tradition that was formerly represented by stick fighters and crude street percussionists, they embellished that identity by adopting romantic military names popularized by American World War II movies. As Stewart observes, "Unlike the *batonniers* of an earlier era who fought with sticks, these bandsmen fought with knives, cutlasses, rocks and razors" (Stewart 1986: 304). Association with a steel band was tantamount to hooliganism until well into the 1960s, and even today the violent clashes of steel bands during carnival continue. In 1983, for example, the closing night of the Trinidad Carnival was marked by a crossroads confrontation of two steel bands. There was one casualty, the victim of a broken bottle that was smashed over his head and then used to cut him to death.

At the same time, the steel band has gained recognition as an ingenious musical invention, reportedly the only percussion instrument ever made which has all the notes of the scale on the same surface. Social approval of the steel band began gradually and hesitantly in the 1950s, when Winston "Spree" Simon developed the practice of having the steel bands play classical, church, and cosmopolitan popular music as well as calypso (Hill, E. 1972: 51). The positive acceptance of steel band continued under the influence of black nationalism in Trinidad, and through the international popularization of carnival. At home and abroad, Trinidadians are fond of citing the steel band as an example of their culture's creative ability to transform a product of industrial waste into an object of artistic expression. The steel band, they claim with justification, is the outstanding musical invention of the twentieth century.

While the steel band is found everywhere that Trinidadians have settled in the metropolitan world, it has had a special affinity to England. It was there in the early 1950s that touring steel bands from Trinidad first gained international recognition. The growing West Indian immigrant population in England were part of that process. For them, the artistic success of the steel band struck the same note as the sporting success of the West Indian cricket team, which was then winning its first victories against England and gradually establishing itself as the outstanding power in world cricket. The two symbols converged when steel bands, touring and later locally-produced, enlivened English cricket grounds with performances celebrating the triumphs of their team.[3]

As steel bands developed within West Indian immigrant communities in England, they also preserved their alternate tradition of violent conflict. The immigrants themselves were overwhelmingly black and primarily involved in unskilled labor, and the conditions of race and class discrimination that they experienced in an increasingly reactionary British society were similar to those that prevailed at the time when the steel bands evolved in late-colonial Trinidad. By the end of the 1950s, when race riots were dramatizing the plight of blacks in Britain, many immigrants were coming to the view that their social condition had worsened—a realization made doubly painful by their earlier dream of finding acceptance and opportunity in the "mother country."

When carnival began in the Notting Hill area of London in 1965, the steel band was its chief performative expression. The carnival parade, particularly after its full Caribbeanization in the early 1970s, consisted primarily of steel bands, a few of which embellished their movement

Disguised as a bird, a masquerader contributes to the visual splendor of the Caribana parade in Toronto. In the background is Queen's Park, seat of the Ontario legislature.

through the streets with small, relatively modest masquerade auxiliaries (Cohen 1980: 71-74). But it was steel bands—not, as in Toronto, the independent masquerade bands—that constituted the basic organizational units.

Cohen also emphasizes the militant symbolism of the steel band as understood by West Indian carnivalists in London. "Here in Britain," one of his activist informants told him, "we need the steel band more than in Trinidad." Another observed, "The steel band was born in violence and it expresses violence" (Cohen 1980: 71-72). A similar view was expressed by Darcus Howe, the editor of *Race Today* and a long-time carnival leader; infuriated by the victimization of West Indians during the Notting Hill carnival, Howe wrote that he had to join one of the bands and spend two or three hours "knocking the hell out of steel" in order to ventilate his anger and regain his emotional equilibrium (Howe 1976: 175).

The steel bands remain the social and symbolic focal point of the Notting Hill carnival. Year after year, the steel bandsmen clash with an almost entirely white police force, who have themselves become ubiquitous and highly ambivalent symbols of the carnival (Cohen 1982). Unsuccessful in their attempts to move carnival into Wembley Stadium, where it could be physically and symbolically contained, the police have sought instead to infiltrate the event and intimidate its participants. On a few occasions—1976 and, more recently, 1987—the annual carnival skirmishes between steel bandsmen and police erupted into riots. More commonly, they are ritualized episodes of social conflict that are contained within the framework of festivity. In all cases, carnival is a public reminder of its own violent origins within the context of race and class oppression, and a public warning that instruments of music and militancy will continue to challenge the authority of the British state, just as they earlier challenged its colonial representation in Trinidad.

Art, Politics, and Celebration

Caribbean entertainment and its accessories—dance and dress styles, food and fashion, argot and art forms—have become commonplace features of urban environments throughout the metropolitan world. As anthropologist and art historian Robert Thompson observes:

In Brooklyn, Toronto, and London taste a star apple/akee/patty/roti; hear in New York salsa/merengue/compas/shanking/soca music; dance in Paris a cadence/compas/reggae/songo/mambo universe in motion....A new art history, a new visual tradition, based on beads and feathers and masks and percussion-dominated street-marchers, permeates certain neighborhoods of our major cities. To repeat: a whole lot of shaking, drumming, chanting, feathering, beading, multi-lappeting, and sequinning is going on. How did it happen? Immigration, mon (Thompson 1988: 17).

In Toronto, Caribana is celebrated by a masquerade band comprised mostly of East Indians from Trinidad.

Thompson does not exaggerate. With two million Caribbean persons—about a quarter of them from the Commonwealth countries, or West Indies—New York is appropriately described as the world's largest Caribbean city (Sutton 1987: 19). Toronto and London are not far behind. In Canada, there are an estimated 320,000 West Indian-born persons, a substantial majority of them living in metropolitan Toronto (Henry 1987: 215). About the same number of West Indians as are now found in Canada came to Britain during the heaviest immigrant influx from the early 1950s through 1962; they and their descendants now number more than half a million persons, with the heaviest concentration in London (Foner 1985: 709).

But more than numbers are involved. Commenting on the adaptive strategies of the West Indian immigrant, Segal underscores a seeming paradox: On the one hand, West Indians resist *assimilation* into the host society, choosing instead to maintain ongoing cultural ties to the Caribbean homeland. On the other hand, they actively seek *integration*, insisting on their "full civic, political, and economic rights and opportunities" (Segal 1987: 47).

The overseas carnivals, the most intense and spectacular manifestation of Caribbean popular culture in the metropolitan world, are centrally relevant to both expressions of this paradox. Aesthetically, they are what Rex Nettleford describes alliteratively as a "salve for the suffering caused by the severance" (Nettleford 1988: 184)—a kind of social therapy that overcomes the separation and isolation imposed by the diaspora and restores to West Indian immigrants both a sense of community with each other and sense of connection to the culture that they claim as a birthright. Politically, however, there is more to these carnivals than cultural nostalgia. They are also a means through which West Indians seek and symbolize integration into the metropolitan society, by coming to terms with the opportunities, as well as the constraints, that surround them.

In each case examined above, carnival can be conceptualized as a phase in a process of transition. In Toronto, West Indians are becoming black Canadians in an affluent, middle-class society in which politics is based on ethnic patronage and multiculturalism enjoys the rhetorical status of a civil religion, circumstances that enable ethnocultural spectacles to claim the respectful attention of the media, the financial support of business, and the sympathy of the general public. In London, West Indians are becoming—and have already become—black Britons, but the process has been very different than in Canada; rigid and oppressive class distinctions persist, the economy has been badly depressed for two decades, and "immigrant" has become a racist code word for non-white. Finally, West Indians in Brooklyn are also, inevitably, becoming black Americans, just as did the earlier generations who settled in Harlem; but in the American context, the factor of black ethnicity is involved, and West Indians evoke it in the carnival milieu to symbolize both their cultural identity and their practical interests.

In all cases carnival remains, *sui generis,* an artistic event, not a political one. But its consummate cultural significance ensures that it will always have political implications and functions. Carnival is what Cohen (1974) terms a two-dimensional public drama, a performance in which cultural and political meanings act upon each other in mutually influential ways. An awareness of this reciprocal interaction illuminates the complexity and profound importance of what is quite possibly the world's most popular transnational celebration.

Chapter Three
A Case Study in Political Resistance:
Antigua Carnival '87

Inga E. Treitler

Introduction

This paper is part of an ongoing study that examines the socio-political dimensions of Antiguan Carnival, and the implications of the observed patterns for the society at large. The use of space in the 1987 Carnival is suggestive of complex social responses to the recent economic development on this Eastern Caribbean island. The assumption upon which this analysis is tentatively based is that there are two ideological systems in conflict. Future research may reveal these systems to be not in conflict, but complementary, however the existence of a dynamic relationship between two idea systems in Carnival, and in the broader society, appears undeniable.[1]

The Carnival space is separated into dichotomous areas characterized by distinctive behaviors, as well as by class distinctions. One area, the Antigua Recreation Grounds, referred to during this season as *Carnival City*, is where the formal competitions are staged. The other, an open field across from Carnival City filled with temporary shacks, where people gather informally to socialize, drink, and gamble, is referred to as *Las Vegas*. The analysis of the activities in these two areas reveal conflicting ideological systems. Las Vegas is populist and suggestive of nostalgia for more traditional times, whereas Carnival City activities are organized around the themes of capitalism, which entail competition, consumerism, and social stratification. These two ideological systems underpin traditional and progressive worldviews respectively, creating a tension in the political culture in this, as in all new nations.

The tension between these systems, exemplified by the use of space, is articulated by the master of ceremonies for the staged Carnival events and by the calypsonians who serve the function of social commentary and cultural critique. These Carnival performers criticize not only Antiguan culture and society, but the very trajectory Carnival has taken.

Analysis of the Carnival Space

37

Carnival City and Las Vegas are located on the main crossroad in the capital city of St. John's, bounded by government and administration on one side, and by centers of trade and commerce on the other. Symbolic anthropologists have long recognized the special significance of crossroads, marketplaces, and other open spaces where commerce predominates. In these spaces, normal patterns of relating may break down because transitoriness allows people to be less accountable for their behavior (Babcock—Abrahams 1975). In such areas of license, where the normative structure loosens its grip, it is easier for the people to act out or articulate their resistance to norms, thus creating alternative programs. It is just this creativity that was observed in Antigua Carnival '87.

Carnival City

Carnival City events are formalized, centrally organized, and characterized by extravagance, conspicuous consumption, glitter, and expensive production and recording equipment. Dress is flashy; flirtation is open; and the sexuality of the audience is an important part of the show. This is the area where calypso, steel band, queen, and talent competitions are judged. Anyone who can pay the entry fee can get in to see the show. Prices are uniform for each event, with the exception of the queen show (the significance of scaled entrance fees for the queen show will be taken up in a future paper).

Two forms of commerce are evident here. Hucksters with trays and coolers ring the area of reserved seating selling cigarettes, peanuts, gum, candy, packaged cookies, and soft drinks. Permanent booths and bars encircling the outer general admission area do brisk business in alcohol, especially beer, rum, and whisky, and some sell traditional fried chicken and fish balls, prepared on the spot and served up with hot sauce and slices of white bread. There is a preference for imported food and drink in this area, which, together with the admission charge, contributes to the commercial orientation here.

The competitions are held on a stage with a background mural that usually celebrates some feature of Antiguan culture. This mural is an important part of the stage performances, because it can hardly be omitted from photographs and videotapes. It is significant therefore, that the murals are inspired increasingly by external, rather than local or regional themes.

Las Vegas

Formerly, games were played in the outer ring of Carnival City where the permanent concession booths are located, but as the festival grew, the area became too congested and these events had to be moved to the wide open field next to the bus station that was once a marketplace. Booth owners in Las Vegas continue to be accountable to the government Carnival Committee, however the required fee appears to vary with political affiliation and other non-economic factors, rather than market forces.

Temporary eight—by—ten foot shacks are brought in on trucks, or constructed on site, as early as a month before Carnival officially starts. They are arranged in a configuration that resembles a village, with narrow "roads" running between them. They are creatively painted and decorated with symbols of the owners' personal style and, in some cases, encircled by low fences with gaming tables for cards or dominoes. Because each establishment carries approximately the same range of products, people tend to patronize friends, kin, and neighbors. Some of these shacks are saved by their owners from year to year, and become functional parts of the traditional house yards between Carnivals. Others are saved for rental to entrepreneurs in future Carnivals.

A cursory glance suggests that participation is predominantly Antiguan, male, and working class. Dominant themes in Las Vegas are local, and the popular drinks are "male" or regional. They include Guinness Stout (a drink associated with masculine potency), Red Stripe Beer (Jamaican), and Cavalier rum (Antiguan). Las Vegas is community oriented, so people tend to patronize friends, kin, and neighbors and booth owners do not need to worry about market forces in the selection of products. As a result, most booths carry the same range of goods. Most food is prepared on the spot, and includes such West Indian favorites as black pudding (seasoned mixture of blood and rice stuffed into an intestine), souse (pig ears and tail, prepared in a seasoned sauce), fried or barbecued chicken, fish balls, black eye peas and rice, and pig foot. The air is heavy with aromas of cooking oil, meat, and seasonings, as well as ganja (i.e., marijuana, that staple of the Rastafarian creed, now popular among the nation's youth).

Carnival and Socio—Political Critique

Carnivals have existed in the Caribbean since the arrival of the French colonists in the 16th century. In Europe, Catholics know *Carnivale* as the "farewell to meat." It is a period of relaxed inhibitions, and a time to celebrate life's carnal pleasures before the abstinence that is Lent. In the Caribbean, Trinidad's Carnival was the first and remains the most elaborate, with retentions not only of the colonial, but also West African and East Indian cultures. The African cultural features have their origin in the societies from which African peoples were forcibly exported in the 16th through the 19th centuries; and the Indian elements are from the indentured laborers who arrived from India during the 19th century. Since the development of the tourist industry in the Caribbean, Carnival has been commercialized in many islands, to the point that in recent years, even nominally Protestant islands have developed carnivals.

Carnivals are not only moments of unbridled joyousness and celebration of life, but also occasions of heightened political self consciousness. In the calypso—that indigenous musical form that has come to be associated with carnivals through the Caribbean—singers cast a metaphorical glance over the state of their nation, world affairs, and the human condition. In these songs, and the public reaction to them, we find an accurate reflection of popular sentiment about social, economic, and political conditions in the nation.

Participants in mass popular celebrations are particularly susceptible to suggestion and social critique. A feeling of solidarity and unity, even ecstasy, prevail, enabling people to share and internalize the ideals expressed by the group. Ordinary rules of behavior are abandoned and participants focus on the ethos of the festivities, whether a sports event, a celebration of independence, or a flea market.

Scholars have noted that the amount of pandemonium and lawlessness created by these festivals varies inversely with the egalitarianism of everyday society (DaMatta 1977). In Brazil, a very class conscious society, *Carnaval* temporarily creates an egalitarian social order, strengthening the individual and empowering the dispossessed. At the other extreme, in New Orleans (an ideologically more egalitarian society), Mardi Gras invents temporary hierarchies and exclusions (DaMatta 1977: 236). The dichotomy between everyday behavior and festival pandemonium can be seen in Antigua, where economic and political restructuring have made the society more competitive. Coincidentally, government rhetoric about Carnival stresses themes of unity: a time to "forget the differences, the bickering and the chasms that seemingly divide us" (*Antiguan Carnival '87*, souvenir pamphlet). The development of a populist ideology within Las Vegas can be seen as a reversal of the growing social stratification.

Cultural Decolonization and Carnival

Carnival festivals the world over are typified by the empowerment of the individual, as manifested in the opportunity to express a desire for specific changes, and in the resistance to the dominant system of values. In Antiguan Carnival 1987, resistance existed at two levels. First, it was a metacommentary in which many opposed the exploitation of the festival by commercial interests; that is, Carnival, itself a form of commentary, took on the function of commenting upon itself. Furthermore, the implications of this metacommentary have relevance for the society at large: at a broader level the festival belongs to the continuing struggle for cultural and political decolonization. In the context of Carnival, the people are expressing disillusionment with the growing commercialization of their culture, as more and more traditional carnival events are sacrificed to the demands of the marketplace. Steelband competitions, for example, cannot be staged unless sponsorship can be retained the year around (Dorbrine Omard, personal communication 1989). Likewise, calypsonians are increasingly dependant on sponsorship, and the criteria set by recording studios take priority over spontaneity and timeliness of composition. In Antiqua, calypsos are increasingly products to be sold on an international market, and have thus lost much of the local flavor that historically defined the musical form.

Because Caribbean peoples were colonized for four centuries, and because the population was not indigenous to begin with, but imported from various parts of Africa and Asia as tools in the growth of European mercantilism, cultural identity in the region has long been a tenuous phenomenon, and political subjugation under various guises has continued to this day despite ongoing popular struggles.

Throughout the colonized world, cultural identity has always been a product of tension and sometimes negotiation between the dominant culture of the power structure, and the culture of the colonized masses. After World War II, as the end of the colonial era approached, the emblem of Great Britain was gradually replaced by that of North America, which, as a magnet for migration, symbolized young peoples' economic aspirations and life goals.

The challenge to the development of a national culture is especially evident in the smaller Caribbean islands, where tourism is effectively a "monocrop," that is, the main focus of the economy, as sugar once was. In addition, the results of the United States expansionary policies can be seen on the cultural landscape. Two prominent features of this influence are the Peace Corps initiative, with its vision of international relations; and the invasion of Grenada, with the imperialist implication of intolerance, especially with regard to relations with Cuba.

The theme of Antigua's 1987 Carnival mural illustrates this trend with a depiction of the island as a service-oriented Mecca for tourists, virtually devoid of human life. An enormous empty swimming pool is bordered by rows of vacant, sun bathed tables, attended by stereotypical handsome, uniformed "natives" ready to serve up tropical drinks. This design stands in marked contrast to the murals and symbols of the 1970s Carnivals, which celebrated Black Power, Pan-Africanism, and national pride (Manning 1978).

Carnival Season in Antigua

Preparation for Carnival, the biggest event of the year, begins as soon as the previous year's events are over. The festivities begin in early July when Calypso "tents" are the main attraction, but formal activities don't start until the last Monday in July, and by the first Tuesday in August, they are over. In July, jam sessions for the calypsonians are staged several nights a week to eliminate all but semi-final competitors before Carnival week, and throughout this month, calypsos are aired back—to—back on the nation's two radio stations.

Carnival is kicked off with staged extravaganzas in which finalists in the steel band, beauty, junior talent, and calypso competitions are selected. The calypso finals run until about 3 a.m. Monday, at which time people spill into night clubs, home, or to a quiet alley to await *jouvert* (pronounced "jouvay," from the French *jour overt,* open day). About 5 a.m. people start arriving downtown for "jump-up," wearing shorts and, in some cases, costumes or placards bearing political slogans. Jump-up begins with the arrival of bands playing winning calypsos and popular favorites. Originally the bands were on foot, and steel drums were carried around the neck on wide leather straps, but today musicians ride floats pulled by tractors, and, to compete with the noise of the tractors, the bands (or recordings) are amplified through enormous speakers. By 10 a.m., the sun is overhead, and people, exhausted from dancing and singing all morning, drift into favorite restaurants for *jouvert* breakfast, and then home or to the beach to rest before the afternoon parade.

Mas' (masquerade) troupes are groups of up to 300 people organized around a variety of traditional and original themes expressed in the costumes and banners. Monday afternoon, these troupes meet at the outskirts of town and parade down the main streets, winding up on the stage of Carnival City, where they are judged for originality of costume. The troupes are sponsored by members of the business community and may celebrate the history of the sponsor's product, such as Milo (a British malted milk drink) or Cavalier Rum (from the local distillery), or they may be thematically organized around such motifs as musical instruments, seasons of the year, Phoenix rising from the flames, African heritage, Old Time Carnival, and stilt walkers and clowns. Winners of the Masquerade are announced on Tuesday afternoon when Mas' troupes once again dance across the stage and then pour into the streets for the "Las' Lap," which might go on until after midnight.

The Performers

The Calypsonian

The attempts by government on the one hand to stress unity, and by Carnival performers and participants on the other, to deemphasize unity and make concessions to a decentralizing movement in the form of the populist Las Vegas, are both subject to comment and critique by the calypsonians. Calypsonians have served the function of social commentary and cultural critique throughout the history of the musical form. In more traditional times, before its affiliation with carnivals, calypso was referred to as the newspaper of the people, and provided an often illiterate population with rapid transmission of information. The use of ambiguous language, *double entendres*, metaphor, and folklore is a feature that has protected the performer from censorship and persecution, and therefore contributed to the music's longevity in repressive societies. It also contributes to the excitement surrounding the many political calypsos, as the performers obliquely criticize the government, or prominent public figures.

A competitor in the 1987 junior competition drew attention to the competitiveness of Antiguans in a song called "Crab Antics." The title refers to the element in the belief system of small scale societies typical of the Anglophone Caribbean, that makes the accumulation of wealth taboo (see Wilson 1973). The metaphor (from folklore) of crabs in a barrel elucidates the behavior of those who, in their struggles to escape, pull others down with them, insuring that all will be condemned to the bottom. Antiguans have been known to describe their society by reference to this metaphor. The calypso's refrain, "push...shove...gotta get ahead..." is about the breakdown of the social proscription that insures equal distribution of wealth, and discourages hoarding. The calypso suggests that the stratification emergent over the last decade has lead to mutual exploitation among Antiguans for the purpose of social and financial advancement.

One of the better known of the senior competitors in 1987 sang about corruption, exploitation of natural resources, and illicit romantic and political *rendezvous*'s in his calypso "De Night de Sun Come Out." These activities all come to light when the sun talks the moon into changing places. The calypsonian argues that Antigua's people prefer to close their eyes to official corruption because, if they position themselves strategically, they might be on the receiving end of the graft some day.

The role of calypso in the critique of culture can also be abused by politicians. It is rumored, for example, that in Carnival 1987, one calypsonian was paid by a government minister to praise the government for the prosperity of the country, and to chastise those calypsonians who criticized their government publicly.

The Emcee

The master of ceremonies in West Indian Carnival celebrations is typically what Roger Abrahams calls a "man of words," (1983), a kind of verbal trickster. Like the calypsonian, he gets away with saying what others cannot say, without fear of retribution. However, unlike the calypsonian, his performance is completely spontaneous. His style is flexible, ranging from the North American disc jockey, to the banter of Antiguan villages, covering the whole "post—creole continuum" (Bickerton 1975). He comments on the performances while technicians struggle with technical difficulties, cracks jokes that predominate with sexual innuendoes and *double entendres*, and gets a terrific response from the crowd.

In Antigua in 1987, the emcee confronted the contradiction between aspirations of the Carnival planners and the actual performances. On the one hand, a glamourous stage was built; admission was charged;

and elaborate high tech sound equipment was purchased by the Carnival Committee, which aspired to a high level of professionalism. On the other hand, however, sound technicians and musicians were late; no one seemed to known how to use the equipment; and the end product was agonizingly ragged.

He chastised the organizers and technicians for their lack of professionalism, effectively transforming the space of Carnival City into a village road where this kind of chastisement and public criticism is the rule (Reisman 1974). He acted out the tension that existed between modernization and tradition—the ambiguous feelings of individuals who switched cultural codes between grandma's souse, and the fast food wolfed down on a work day. In his banter, he parodied the anger of many Antiguans witnessing the loss of tradition to American imports; yet, he pointed out that these same individuals would go to all lengths to purchase the products seen on cable television that are now symbols of success in Antigua. Following a particularly slick rendition of an American pop song, he sighed mockingly "doesn't that make you want to run out and get a 'Big Mack'?"

Critique and open commentary are the first steps in resolving cultural conflicts, such as the tension between the desire to protect traditional culture and the desire for economic advancement. As in many societies with repressive structures, there is a need in Antigua for popular participation in such critique. Carnival is a temporary release from the normative structure and provides the forum. Las Vegas is used as a commentary (or more precisely, a metacommentary) on the commercialization of Carnival, that becomes public dialogue when articulated by the festival's spokespeople—the calypsonians and the master of ceremonies who, judging from the active crowd participation, represent public concern. By looking at these performances as metaphors, it can be said that there is a general critique of the social consequences of recent economic development in Antigua.

The Background

The key historical background to this economic development is the replacement of agriculture by tourism as the mainstay of the Antiguan economy. With the restructuring of the economy, living conditions have improved markedly over the last five years for the majority of the working class. However, this improvement has not been without negative consequences, because, although tourism provides valued jobs for Antiguans, the integrity of the local culture is threatened by the pressures of the largely foreign controlled tourism—based economy. Many Antiguans are concerned about the exploitation of cultural resources as devices for tourist marketing.

Formerly, Antigua was one of Britain's typical sugar islands with good production levels, occasionally as high as those of St. Kitts and Barbados, the biggest producers. Today, Antigua gains 80 percent of earned foreign exchange from tourism as compared to only 1 percent from agriculture.

Antigua, with 108 square miles, is one of the larger Leeward islands, and with a population of 78,000, is among the more densely occupied countries on earth. Modern life styles make it impossible for this number of people to be supported by local resources, so the island is dependent on the outside world for imported products, investment capital, and earned income. The majority of Antiguans are descendants of the West African slaves who were imported as labor for the sugar plantations. The remaining 10—15 percent are descendants of British, Portuguese, Syrian, and Lebanese immigrants and North American and European pensioners.

Political History

As elsewhere in the English—speaking Caribbean, Antigua's political history is intimately connected to the labor and trade union movements that swept the region in the 1930s. The first union, the Antigua Trades and Labour Union (AT & LU), gained credibility among the working people by winning a 50 percent increase in all daily wages within a year of its registration in March 1940. Membership rose dramatically, and it was through trade unionism that organized popular political activity began (Henry 1985: 87). The mass appeal of unions was largely, though not exclusively, a function of their negotiations with the planters, who were then the biggest employers on the islands, since an independent peasantry never developed and there was no industry to speak of (Henry 1985: 50).

The early struggles of the labor union were largely village—based, with many villages organizing local union branches that were able to reach a broad base of the population. This grassroots political activity provided an important foundation for the political developments of the 1950s and 1960s.

Village—based, mutual aid societies provided basic structures from which protest movements could develop. These societies existed among the workers in many Caribbean islands from as far back as the turn of the 18th century (before emancipation). They were organized on egalitarian principles and had the function of providing financial and social support systems for their members, in addition to serving political purposes, since they were the only mass organizations available (Henry 1985: 82). By the 1950s, when union activity was well underway, extensive political debate characterized all levels of society, bolstering the struggles for independent statehood, which was achieved in 1967. These decades were characterized by the unity of purpose among Antigua's working people, to which the contemporary opposition movements are harkening with nostalgia.

Economic Change

The transition to a tourism—based economy was stimulated by the opening of the U.S. military base in 1941. American servicemen and their families returned home with the news that Antigua was an attractive place to visit. The island was "discovered" shortly thereafter by tourists and North American and European investors. The opening of tourist hotels in Antigua also came at an opportune time to profit from the Cuban revolution in 1959, which forced the closing of U.S. - owned and - patronized hotels.

The dredging of a shipping harbor in 1968, and the expansion of the airport to receive jumbo jets, improved Antigua's prospects as a tourist island (and happily so because the sugar industry had entirely collapsed by 1972). Cruise ships bringing tourists began counting Antigua as a stop on their Caribbean cruises, and jumbo jets brought travellers from other islands, North America, and Europe. The perennial drought conditions that have long undermined agricultural efforts, proved a boon for tourism, as North Americans and Europeans wishing to escape the dreary, wet winters at home, sought rain—free days in the warm sun.

Between 1950 and 1970, the number of beach hotels increased from one to nineteen (Dyde 1986: 35). By 1985 there were 37 hotels, 19 guest houses, and 39 apartment units, for a total of 98 tourist establishments providing accommodations for 300,000 per year, several times the national population. Today, young Antiguans rely on jobs in various sectors of the tourist economy: hotels, restaurants, airport, local transportation, construction, banking and commerce. Antiguan—initiated entrepreneurship, long handicapped by a shortage of capital, is on the rise.

It was not only tourism that benefitted from improved connections with the outside world. The industrial sector also made significant advances enhanced by foreign investment. Today, Antigua possesses several plants that assemble clothing, mattresses, furniture, and electronic components, and produce such commodities as soft drinks, chemical products, and rum for local and regional markets. The 1985 Statistical Yearbook reports 4.45 percent of GDP from manufacturing, 11.87 percent from wholesale and retail trade, and 6.27 percent from banks and insurance.

The increased amount of money that has been brought into circulation by the changes outlined in this section, gives the island the look of a boom economy. Highly visible are the new housing, new stores, new cars, and new road work. All this newness only begs the question of who controls the money that pays the bills. Indications of indebtedness, both individual and national, appear in newspapers when banks sell the cars they repossess, and foreign investors buy national luxury hotels that are sold in attempts to clear the national debt.

Antigua's working people have experienced major changes in a single generation. On the one hand, economic growth has triggered upward mobility within all social classes, and material benefits are within reach for many people for the first time. But, on the other hand, the island has experienced a veritable invasion of tourists and foreign investors about whom Antiguans have mixed feelings. Whereas officially—in the media and political addresses—tourists are welcomed; unofficially, in private, many Antiguans resent these guests. Some, like author, Jamaica Kincaid, express anger because the nation's well-being depends on transforming the island into a playground for the North American and European middle and upper classes.

Conclusions

The economic and political changes that began with the transformation from a sugar—based to a tourism—based economy, and with the shift from the British colonial domination to that by North American enterprise, has resulted in the emergence of a dominant capitalist ideology in Antigua. In turn, the dominance of this ideology manifests social and cultural changes that are disturbing to many Antiguans. There is considerable ambivalence in the face of recent economic growth because, whereas everyone can appreciate the opportunity these changes have brought, unfortunate alliances between North American and European investors and Antiguan ministers of government do nothing to diminish the appearance of official corruption.

In this paper it is seen that a populist ideological system has crystallized in response to recent economic development and appears to be in opposition to the dominant idea system. This populist ideology is expressed in Las Vegas, an unofficial center of Carnival activity opposite Carnival's official center, and is indicative of efforts by some Antiguans to repatriate Carnival (and by extension, Antiguan culture), i.e., to regain control from government, which in turn is subject to North American demands. The performances of calypso singers and of the masters of ceremonies articulate both ideological systems and acknowledge the tension that exists between them.

It has been suggested throughout this paper that the two ideological systems at work in Carnival are in conflict. This paper is part of an ongoing study, and future research may reveal these to be not in conflict but complementary, functioning in tandem to generate alternative programs, whether through popular culture, or through direct political action.

Chapter Four
"Is We Carnival:" Cultural Traditions
Under Stress in the U.S. Virgin Islands

Klaus de Albuquerque

Introduction

It has become increasingly common to view Caribbean carnivals, both local and overseas, as part of the popular culture, an unfortunate development, since the implied dichotomy between high and low culture suggested by the term popular culture has all but disappeared in the English-speaking Caribbean.

Admittedly, the Trinidad Carnival (the forerunner of most modern-day Caribbean carnivals) did have rather genteel origins but was later taken over by the masses (Pearse 1971) before effective control over the organization of carnival eventually passed into the hands of the middle class. Today, this class continues to control the organization of most Caribbean carnivals through carnival committees and the like, and carnival itself has been transformed into a broad-based national (even regional) festival representative of a cultural tradition rich in music, dance, and festive cuisine.

Manning (1978) suggests that many small-island carnivals, originally established to bolster tourism in the slow summer season, have taken on a nativistic quality and have become, as it were, exercises in cultural revitalization that serve to counter-balance the insidious Americanization (through cable television, mass tourism, retirement colonies of affluent Americans, etc.) so prevalent in the region.

Nowhere is this Americanization more intense than in the U.S. Virgin Islands (USVI), and it is here, that carnival, rather than serving as a cultural safety valve, actually exacerbates the existing tensions fostered by political and economic dependence, by reminding black Virgin Islanders that no area of their life is free from the crass intrusions of their political masters. And crass these intrusions are, since white expatriate participation in Carnival through troupes, floupes, inappropriate costumes, and non-West Indian themes, undermines the spirit of Carnival as a celebration of Virgin Islands cultural identity and West Indian solidarity. It is not surprising, therefore, that "is we carnival" (it is our carnival) is the oft-heard rallying cry of a beleaguered minority seeking to preserve their cultural patrimony.

Historical Background

In 1917, the United States bought the Virgin Islands from Denmark for $25 million. The decision to purchase these islands, which many naval personnel called a "damn bunch of rocks" (Knud-Hansen 1947: 100) and which President Herbert Hoover was to dub an "effective poorhouse of practically no value to the United States" (Evans 1945: 289), was based solely on strategic/geopolitical concerns. The U.S. Navy, which was put in charge of administering them, went about the task of "rehabilitating" the islands by concentrating their efforts largely on public health and the infrastructure, to the neglect of the economy. Not surprisingly, at the end of the Navy's stewardship, one critical observer was to note that the USVI were "what they had been for many years, a land and a people so firmly caught in the grip of economic forces" (Evans 1945: 2) that they could only carry on with outside aid.

With the appointment of the first civilian governor in 1931, the U.S. government embarked on a major program of economic rehabilitation of the islands, the cornerstone of which was the homestead project whereby large estates would be purchased and broken up into small plots for resale to would-be farmers. The new governor and his administrators proceeded with great energy to promote basket weaving and needle work cooperatives, provide seeds, cuttings, and garden plots, plant trees and so on, believing that all that was needed was a critical quantum of resources to propel the USVI economy across the threshold into its own pattern of self-sustained growth (McElroy and de Albuquerque 1984: 48). But more money, more laws, a hotel project, and the purchase of estates for homesteading, did not provide the needed impetus. Although some observers (Evans 1945: 313-315) attempted to place the blame on the character of Virgin Islands people (their "unwillingness to work" and their "inefficiency") and on "misguided labor leaders and politicians," what most observers failed to realize was that USVI development problems were not internal and that the territorial economy was not a *sui generis* system, functioning in relative isolation from the mainland economy. Furthermore, to expect a tiny, resource—poor group of islands—whose people had few technical skills given the Danish orientation towards education—to achieve self-sufficiency as measured by U.S. mainland standards, was sheer folly.

In the 1940s and 1950s, the U.S. federal government, undaunted by previous failure, continued to push for self-sufficiency, and while the policies varied (civil service reform, specific grants-in-aid to overcome problems and bottlenecks, fiscal austerity, etc.) from one governor and federal administrator to another, the deficits continued, and along with them, dependence on the federal government.

In the 1960s, the long-awaited economic turn-around finally arrived because of a fortuitous combination of both external and internal factors. The former included the U.S. embargo of Cuba which diverted U.S. tourists and capital to the islands, the advent of jet aircraft which reduced travel time from the mainland, and an elastic low-cost labor supply from the nearby Leeward and Windward Islands. The internal factors involved the "aggressive implementation of a broad array of growth policies by local officials," namely, the phase-out of commercial sugar production, the creation of an industrial incentive program, and most importantly, aggressive lobbying in Washington (McElroy and de Albuquerque 1984: 50). Realizing that the USVI had significant tourism potential, Washington began to underwrite the massive infrastructure program that was necessary to support the large scale modernization of the USVI economy. In addition, Washington began to promote the USVI as the "showplace of democracy" in the Caribbean and as the "American Paradise."

The economy responded by growing at a phenomenal rate. Real gross territorial product grew 10 percent per year, per capita income increased four-fold, tax revenues rose over seven times, the stock of housing more than doubled, and electricity and water consumption rose an average of 20 percent per annum (de Albuquerque and McElroy 1982). During the early 1970s, the economy stagnated a little, but since 1978, it has posted modest gains with noticeable increases in per capita income and retail sales. From 1984, the tourist industry has shown renewed vigor and a number of new hotels have been completed, with still more in progress or on the drawing board. Real estate values and rentals have soared to dizzying heights, effectively shutting out the majority of young adult Virgin Islanders from home ownership.

This economic miracle has not been without its social costs, the most pernicious of which has been the Americanization of the Virgin Islands. Begun originally with the introduction of U.S. mainland education curriculum into the schools, it progressed to colonization of the islands by whites (early white in-migrants saw themselves as "settlers" and published a "Settler's Handbook" as a guide for new and prospective migrants), and the gradual shifting of control of the local economy from a white and near-white elite native class to a new elite of white mainland entrepreneurs. Non-native control of the economy has resulted in a significant increase in the white U.S. born population. In 1917, 7.4 percent of the population was classified as white and only 2.3 percent were born in the mainland U.S. By 1960, the white population rose to 16.7 percent, and in 1987, estimates placed it at close to 19 percent mainland U.S. By 1960, the white population rose to 16.7 percent, and in 1987, estimates placed it at close to 19 percent. Add to this another 1.2 million or so white visitors from the continental U.S., and the white presence in the USVI is everywhere and often overwhelming. Even the political sphere, long a preserve of native Virgin Islanders, is beginning to show the effects of white economic control and demographic presence. For example, in 1986, more native and continental whites were elected to the unicameral legislature than in any other previous election.

It is not surprising that many USVI institutions are under siege and that Virgin Islands culture, which is arguably Afro-West Indian, survives only barely, and largely in the form of cuisine, despite the heroic efforts of many individuals to maintain, revive, and promote it. Now, one of the last surviving institutions, Carnival, is under threat and is in danger of losing its authenticity, or even worse, being suspended, because the level of violence during Carnival has escalated. In fact, following incidents of racial violence during an impromptu tramp on the last day of the 1987 Carnival, numerous prominent Virgin Islanders, including the director of tourism, called for the indefinite suspension of Carnival. That the suspension of Carnival would be bruited about, points to the very precarious state of cultural traditions in the USVI. But before I explore the theme of cultural traditions under stress, I would like to briefly examine the history of Carnival in the USVI.

History of Carnival in the USVI

Carnival in the USVI is synonymous with Carnival in St. Thomas held during the end of April. St. Croix has annual Christmas festivities and St. John its July 4 celebrations-both of which are now being referred to as carnivals.

The origin of Carnival in St. Thomas is fairly well established. In 1912, the first Carnival was organized by a white and near white elite and held on Valentine's Day. A Casilda Durloo was chosen as Carnival queen, one of her pages being Ralph Paiewonsky, who, in 1961, became governor of the USVI. The activities lasted for a 24 hour period (4 a.m. to 4 a.m.) and featured a parade with participants dressed as Zulus, Indians, Cowboys, and Elick the Bear. The next Carnival, held in 1914, expanded to two days and included donkey races, boat races, pie catching contests, and a parade with various troupes and bamboula dancers.[1] The advent of World War I, the transfer of the islands to the U.S., and the subsequent Americanization of the islands, combined to spell the demise of Carnival. Probably the American presence was the overriding factor in the suppression of Carnival, since the early naval administrators and later civilian governors were quite racist in their attitudes and tried to eradicate anything "native."

In 1952, 38 years later, Carnival was revived as a Labor Day (August 31-September 2) celebration, through the efforts of two prominent Virgin Islanders-Ron de Lugo and Eldra Shulterbrandt. The ostensible reason for its revival was to promote/bolster tourism. Although previous American administrations had tried to discourage Virgin Islands folk tradition in music and dance, the three-day affair proved an enormous success with the themes of the two earlier carnivals (1912 and 1914) everywhere apparent. The parade featured troupes of Zulus, Indians, cowboys, bamboula dancers, big heads, and "mocko jumbies" (costumed men on stilts), and various popular bands including "Spooner's Fungi" band (a string band) and the "Gravediggers Orchestra." Special events included demonstrations of quadrille, block dances, a lancers dance, and the traditional mock battle between Zulus and Indians. Soon after 1952, Carnival was shifted to a three-day period toward the end of April in an attempt to extend the tourist season into the month of May. In the early 1960s, Carnival expanded officially to a week, while the season itself now took up most of the month of April. By 1969, the Queen's Ball (the official start of the Carnival season) had been moved back to late March.

In the 1970s, Carnival got very much larger, especially with the inclusion of a wider variety of non-traditional activities. These new activities, the expanded program, and the increasing presence and participation of whites in what had been heretofore a primarily black West Indian celebration, began to change the character of Carnival. Nowhere has this changing character been more noticeable than in the July 4, St. John Carnival. Here increasing white presence in the food stalls at Carnival Village has been noticeable over the years and continental white participation in troupes and floupes has visibly increased, including, the appearance of almost all-white troupes (the "Misfits" in the 1987 Carnival) often inappropriately accompanied by white, rock, Jimmy Buffet-style bands. The latter invariably provoke harsh reproach from black Virgin Islanders, the most frequently heard comment being a proprietary "is we carnival."

The gradual transformation of the St. John Carnival into a kind of continental version of the West Indian bacchanal has been inevitable and has simply paralleled the increasing demographic,[2] economic, and political importance of whites on St. John. It is no wonder that black Virgin Islanders (native and naturalized) fear, and indeed see, a parallel development in the St. Thomas Carnival. While there has always been fairly small white participation (mostly native elite) in the St. Thomas Carnival, in the 1970s and 1980s, many white continentals, particularly long-term residents, joined long-established troupes like the "Raunchy Bunch." What occurred here is very much part of the larger phenomenon of continental white desire for inclusion and acceptance, predicated as

An "Unadulterated" troupe—St. Thomas Carnival

Mocko Jumbies—St. Thomas Carnival

it is on the mistaken notion that long term residence somehow confers de facto native status and brings with it the necessary creolization. The appearance of fairly white troupes (e.g. the "No—Nonsense" troupe) in the St. Thomas Carnival, all the teeth sucking opprobrium notwithstanding, is clearly a harbinger of things to come.

Native Virgin Islanders, and indeed, all black residents of the USVI, feel threatened not only demographically (in 1980, native born Virgin Islanders constituted only 47.2 percent of the population), economically, and increasingly, politically, but also culturally. Confined to low—paying wage jobs, often denied beach access and traditional use of coastal resources, unable to afford land, housing, and the high cost of living, Virgin Islanders have become an embattled minority. For many, Carnival is the last vestige of something authentically native and it too is threatened. Under these circumstances, greater white presence and participation in Carnival is simply a recipe for violence. Although one might argue that the racial violence that occurred in the 1987 Carnival was probably misdirected at innocent bystanders, the roots of the violence go deep and are clearly understandable.

Cultural Traditions Under Stress and Carnival Violence

In recent years, the St. Thomas Carnival has been increasingly plagued by violence. In 1986, a safari bus laden with white tourists was set upon by some youths in the vicinity of Carnival Village. Seen at that time as an aberration perpetrated by "anti-social elements" in the community, the authorities were nevertheless ready for a reoccurrence of violence in 1987. Police reinforcements were brought over from St. Croix and strict time limits and rules were set down for nightly tramps and for J'ouvert (the morning of the children's parade is heralded by a tramp beginning at dawn on Veterans Drive in Charlotte Amalie). Nevertheless, on the last night of Carnival, an impromptu, unauthorized tramp along the Charlotte Amalie waterfront resulted in a trail of terror for a dozen or so whites, many of whom were attempting to drive through the dancing crowd, and two East Indian couples. White victims claimed to have been taunted and attacked by black youths, still in costumes from the earlier Adult's Parade, yelling "kill the white rabbit" and wielding sticks, whips, and bottles. In the week that followed, numerous whites came forward to report racial incidents where they were taunted with the refrain (kill the "white" rabbit) from the popular song ("Legal") by Eddie and the Movements. The USVI community reacted, predictably, in "surprised" outrage at this apparent racial rampage, and attempts at explaining the violence dominated the news and public debate for several weeks.

The police were inevitably blamed for not having enough men on duty on the last night of Carnival. The major blame, however, was levelled at band leader Eddie Francis, and band members were accused of inciting youth with the line in "Legal," their road march entry, where "kill the rabbit" (widely interpreted to mean "kill the *white* rabbit") is repeated three times. The lyrics of the song are reproduced in their entirety below since they reveal a lot about the organization of Carnival, the attempt to control the bands and their followers, the plight of calypsonians, and the social strains so evident in USVI society.

Legal

De Say de Jam Band too rude, dey say we are too rough
Dey say our crowd is too crude, and dey never get enough
We cause confusion last year, we ruin de carnival
So this year you complaining, for a legal bacchanal

Chorus

No more kick and thumbing (Legal)
No more fight and stealing (Legal)
Legal, legal that is how you want de bacchanal
No more throwing elbow (Legal)
No more mashing big toe (Legal)
Legal, legal that is how you want de carnival
All you want is dance in a circle, spin all around
Do a two-step when you come into town
Dos se doe when you in front de stand
Take a bow than wave up yo hand
Who say we wild? It's just Jam Band style.
Boom, boom, bam, bam all inside de Jam Band
Hands in the air, leh me know you're out there
Jump, jump, jump, jump
Kill the rabbit, kill the rabbit, kill the rabbit
Kill Seventeen, kill Seventeen, kill Seventeen

De system raise our taxes, although our money small
Senators get their raises, government workers still bawl
You think it hard to give dem their raise in pay
And still you want to cut back on government holiday

Second Chorus

Our blood pressure rising (Legal)
From de things that you doing (Legal)
Legal, legal, still you want us come out legal
Be on good behavior (Legal)
For your tourist dollar (Legal)
Legal, legal, that is how you want de bacchanal
Record and T-shirt selling, on these you put a ban
No more selling in de parade, or in de stadium
Musicians can't make a dollar you squeezing them dem too
We are tired of you people, telling us what to do

Calypsonians recorded last year, this year can't make again
Nobody to help them, our culture down the drain
You always want to take out, but never putting in
And still you have the heart, to tell us what to sing
(Eddie and the Movements 1987)

The reference to "Jam Band Style," the band's 1986 Carnival hit, was to remind people that the band had been unfairly linked to violence in the 1986 Adult's Parade, because of the song's "mash dem on their big toe" refrain. In 1987, and through their song "Legal," the band wanted to convey their desire to keep everything legal, even though they felt that the proprietary members of society did not hold themselves to the same set of standards. "Kill the rabbit" was variously interpreted by band members to mean do away with negativeness and unfair practices. The "rabbit" refers to other local bands in the competition, and "kill" to metaphorically beating bands such as "Seventeen Plus" in the Carnival competition for favorite tune. In complaining about the finger pointing at "The Movements" as nothing more than an attempt to find a convenient scapegoat, one band member pointedly noted that Carnival violence was a by-product of the tremendous inequalities in USVI society.

Other explanations proffered for the 1987 rampage, including those by a class of tenth graders at the Charlotte Amalie High School, were very telling. They implicated the USVI government for not raising wages sufficiently and for not doing enough to meliorate the high cost of living, especially, in the area of housing and food. They complained about the number of businesses owned by recent white in-migrants, and the reluctance on the part of these businesses to hire locals. Lastly, they railed against the youth of today, their lack of parental discipline, their disinterest in work (this was blamed on the shortage of well-paying jobs for young people), and their destruction by drugs. Some wiser heads, careful not to sound as apologists for the violence, suggested that the situation was probably exacerbated by whites attempting to drive through the crowd, rather than simply pulling over and stopping. Such behavior does demonstrate a certain amount of cultural insensitivity, and viewed in the context of USVI society must be seen as provocative. The *St. Thomas Daily News* columnist, Dana Orie, in a pensive mood, wondered aloud why "the only time we notice the poor and the young is when they get crazy" (Orie 1987: 6).

Although racial violence in the 1987 Carnival prompted a lot of talk about vigilantism, including a *Daily News* editorial suggesting that violence only begets violence, the net result was that during the 1988 Carnival season, whites stayed away in droves from Carnival events, with many choosing to leave St. Thomas for the duration of Carnival. More than a few Virgin Islanders reported that the 1988 Carnival was like

The Charlotte Amalie High School Steel Band—St. Thomas Carnival

McDonalds invades the—St. Thomas Carnival

The Raunchy Bunch's refreshment truck—St. Thomas Carnival

Carnival Costume—1978—St. Thomas Carnival

an "old timey" Carnival-smaller, more authentic, with fewer strident songs, and a very significantly reduced white presence. Unfortunately, changes seen in the 1988 Carnival are only temporary, since demographic and economic pressures will eventually transform Carnival into a commercial, sanitized version of the traditional West Indian cultural extravaganza, to be dished up to white visitors as an added attraction in an increasingly competitive tourist market.

Conclusion

One of the most telling lines in the song "Legal" is "nobody to help them (calypsonians), our culture down the drain." Certainly any examination of USVI history will show that the Americanization of the islands has occurred at the expense of Virgin Islands culture, and as a very small community, the islands have been unable to resist the inevitable transformation of the society that has accompanied mass tourism. The result has been the kind of cultural death in exchange for "tourist dollar" lamented in "Legal."

One may argue that many small island carnivals are functioning to revitalize local culture; however, the fate of these carnivals will surely parallel that of the St. Thomas Carnival, as they become increasingly commercialized and marketed to tourists, and as the non-West Indian population in these islands increases. Perhaps it is time for island governments to realize that Carnival, like any other cultural resource, needs to be carefully protected and nurtured.

Chapter Five
Recording Artists in Jamaica:
Payola, Piracy and Copyright

Marlene Cuthbert
and
Gladstone Wilson

I won't compromise with the system. I know I'm good. But I'm not going through nobody again. I'll sit down until I can get help to do it alone.

Those words illustrate the pain of a Jamaican recording artist who had an international hit but felt severely burned by the recording industry. This chapter begins with a case study of such a musician. The next section, on payola, details responses given by 26 Jamaican musicians when they were asked how local musicians get their music on radio/TV. The third section deals with piracy and includes results from interviews with prominent people in the Jamaican recording industry. Since adequate copyright laws are at least a partial solution to the pain and problems raised in the chapter, the final section describes the copyright situation in Jamaica and the Caribbean.

The survey data used in this chapter are a small part of the data gathered from 26 Jamaican recording artists in 1986 by the writers and two research assistants. The survey was part of a study of the music industry and the potential for the retention of cultural diversity in an age of global communication conducted by the International Communication and Youth Culture Consortium (ICYC), a crosscultural group of researchers from 25 countries.[1]

Case Study

Vincent Morgan

Vincent Morgan is a thirty-six year old singer who makes his living performing with a group called "Stone Fire" in Ocho Rios, a tourist town on the north coast of Jamaica. He grew up in Linstead in central Jamaica, son of a baker and primary school teacher. He began to make music from before he can remember, at least as early as age three. His mother was a Sunday School teacher and he loved music in the church, especially singing with his three brothers in the Gospel Hall choir.

At age 16, he learned to play drums by setting up some barrels. Then he tied the top of a barrel to his legs and used a pair of sticks he had cut to play this "drum." He is entirely self-taught, and because popular music isn't Christian, didn't receive encouragement from his parents. In high school he found that musical education was limited to Tchaikovsky and that the school taught "nothing of our type of music." Hence in the last year of high school, he says, "music took me out of school because I don't love anything more than music."

Vincent loves all kinds of music but would like to arrange "real classical reggae songs, not just for dancing but for listening." Locally, he has been influenced by Jimmy Cliff but, above all, by Bob Marley. He admires Marley because he paid attention to "writing songs and having lyrics that depict real meaning." Internationally, the greatest influence has come from three Americans, Gene Cooper, Otis Redding, and Aretha Franklyn. He also learned a lot about arrangements from American music.

Vincent feels strong links with his African ancestry and notes the clear connection of Jamaican musicians with Africa, especially as seen in the use of the drums. He believes Jamaicans should be proud of where their ancestors came from and should be singing about the experiences they have gone through. He finds no conflict between his fundamentalist Christian upbringing and the Rastafarianism from which reggae came. In his words:

Rastafarians, Christians, all are based on the same thing; there is one God; people call him by different names, but there is one God regardless of race, etc. Is God teach us to make music.

In a period of sixteen years, Vincent has played with three groups, including the "Stone Fire" band, which he joined in 1985, when it was started by Keith Foote, the creative Jamaican owner of "The Little Pub" who took a previous band on tour to Germany.

"Stone Fire," a group of four musicians and singers, plays for six nights a week, four hours a night, at "The Little Pub," one of the most popular venues for both tourists and locals in Ocho Rios. Two band members play instrumental only and two others, including Vincent who plays keyboard, both sing and play. The band plays dinner music first, then more lively music for dancing. Vincent arranges about 50 percent of their music. The band must cater to tourists with songs such as "Yellow Bird," "Big Big Bamboo" and "Matilda," as well as with international soft music, and some reggae and soca from Trinidad. Thus Vincent isn't able to focus on his own kind of reggae music. He says he has to compromise because of the demands of the marketplace and the audience; he wouldn't get a job unless he performed what tourists like.

The group is paid an amount agreed upon in advance. The members of the band have their own instruments—lead guitar, bass guitar, trap set and keyboard, but the club manager doesn't want to pay to rent their instruments, so they use instruments he provides. The sound equipment is owned by the manager and the band members take care of sound and lighting themselves. The group wears white outfits which cost them about $50 each.

All members of the group belong to the Jamaica Federation of Musicians, and Vincent believes the union protects musicians in tourist industry jobs. He added that on tours it's better to be a union member as "it makes you legal."

The group has not yet made a recording but has already produced a video in its role of backup group to "The Mighty Digger" show, an "Afro Caribic Musical Extravaganza," produced twice a week by the club manager. They expect to produce a recording with the same show.

Between 1970 and 1976, Vincent, as a member of a band called "Soul Defenders," made several recordings while working at Coxanne's, one of the oldest Jamaican recording studios. The group had no contract and no lawyer and the recordings, of course, were not copyrighted. Two recordings were released in the United States without the knowledge of the band. Vincent learned about this when he travelled to the U.S. where people told him of hearing his music and showed him the labels. (One recording was on the label Money Disc). Further, a deejay at a radio station invited him for an interview because he knew songs that Vincent and the group had recorded. Vincent was no longer working with Coxanne's and has had no remuneration for the music played and sold abroad.

The "Soul Defenders" were "ripped off" a second time when an Englishman took them to Britain and, among other things, the BBC produced a video of the group. They were told that they would receive $50 every time the video was used, but they had no contract and can only assume that the Englishman is pocketing the proceeds.

Vincent later had problems with another Jamaican studio, Treasure Isles, owned by Sonja Pottinger. His group did songs on her label and then saw some of the songs in the U.S. while visiting there. On the positive side, Vincent has written songs for other artists, including a Jamaican woman who sings in Canada, and has been paid for these.

Vincent's aim is to write and arrange classical reggae songs for good singers so as to succeed on the international scene. He wants to "sing about roots and to the oppressed people, not just in Jamaica." He has songs and singers but not the finances to proceed. And he complained about the payola that is necessary at both radio stations and record shops.

His past experience has been disillusioning and has made him wary about the music business.

He concludes that,

To get play we must have copyright. Our music is gold, but we don't seem to know it. Some countries have natural gold and silver, and we have reggae and we aren't mining it properly.

Payola, Bribes and Other Techniques

Jamaica has two radio stations, JBC-AM and FM and RJR-AM and FM, and one television station, JBC-TV. The Jamaica Broadcasting Corporation (JBC) is a statutory corporation owned by the government and operates on semi-commercial lines. Radio Jamaica (RJR) was begun by Rediffusion of England but is now cooperatively owned by a cross-section of Jamaican organizations, the government, and RJR workers. The island has no cable television so television is limited to one channel on the JBC.

Jamaican music is played on radio stations daily. Twenty-one of the 26 artists interviewed responded to an open ended question about how they get their music played on radio.

As Table 1 indicates, equal numbers (ten artists) stated as their first or second choice that they took the record to the station, used contacts, or used bribes and payola. One artist said his/her promoter or manager got the music played. We can reasonably assume that some artists did not want to admit using payola, so it is likely that numbers for payola are larger. Some specific, and often emotional, responses to how they get their music played on radio were as follows:

"Payola."

"You have to pay money to the disc jockeys due to the corruption found at radio stations. You bribe them to play the records."

"You must send a record to the station and know someone who will help you; it's not in Jamaica alone..."

"Reaching number one doesn't mean number one in quality of record. If the producer has money he can back the record. So better songs aren't played because of this. THE PEOPLE WITH MONEY CAN SET UP A SONG; if I put out ten and buy back five it reaches the charts right away and gets played on radio and everybody buys it."

"Songs with merit are often not played; Bob Marley's songs were played here mainly after they sold internationally. Only when he died, did everyone play his music at dance halls. Most producers don't know about music. Marley didn't deal with bribes."

"Pay the DJs." (two artists)

Table 1

How Jamaican Artists Get Music Played on Radio (N=26)

Means Used	1st Choice		2nd Choice	
	No.	%	No.	%
Taking record or tape to station	8	31	2	
Contacts	6	23	4	15
Payola, bribes	6	23	4	15
Other	1	4	—	—
No answer	5	19	16	6

"I have a warning for the super DJs. Records make people immortal; if people see stupidness on records that is a problem. Everybody wants to record and DJs abuse this. The serious composers can't get their records in the system."

"Some songs don't deserve to be on radio. Our artists want to write, arrange and sing, do everything! I used to write songs for good singers, because not all of them can write and arrange reggae."

"Money is the whole thing. If I had my way I would produce young artists and beat the system. The Ministry of Culture should provide support for us."

"You meet the DJs through a friend, buy them presents. One record company bought the DJ a $10,000 car."

"Try to know the DJ. Give him a record to play at home and hope he liked you and what he hears. Send $20 or $200 and he'll remember you, especially if you promise that in two weeks there's more from where that came from. With two or three free air plays and two more for pay by then you know if the market is responding or not."

"It's hard to get on radio unless you know the DJ and/or pay him. Most guys record and studios do promotions."

"To get aired you have to pay; if the DJ chooses the record you pay him alone; if it's not him alone, you have to pay library people too. Some returns on record sales are less than the DJ is paid."

"Drop off three or more copies to RJR and JBC radio with a note to the DJ. Contact him, asking him to give it some air time. If this doesn't work, then pay someone to push the effort."

"Submit to the stations—some people pay bribes."

"By knowing a disc jockey or someone at the radio stations to help push the record by frequent playing."

"By flooding records to radio stations, and by payola. Carry several copies to the radio stations and distribute the records to each and every disc jockey and then you give payola to each one of them according to the popularity of their radio shows. The bigger the DJ, the more money you pay."

"By taking records to the particular radio stations and paying the librarians who in turn review them and, if worthy for air, they play them."

"You have to be shrewd to get a record on the airwaves. I understand you have to pay to be played more than usual."

"By contacts, famous or otherwise. Other artist give five 45s to DJs and hope they will play it. If the DJ personally doesn't like your record, take a 45 to someone who knows someone at the station and pay a DJ."

"Usually give a radio station a complimentary copy and they will play it and people will buy it. Then give it to disco men and people hear it and then buy it. Greasing the palm is very common, but the DJ will never admit it."

Only three respondents made neutral comments and the last two quotations are from people who haven't produced records.

"Try taking five copies to the DJ at the radio station. Wait two weeks for them to assess it; then you might hear it once or twice. If it's a 'bad' (very good) shot, they play it a lot."

"Copies of records are sent to stations."

"Give copies to radio stations and give video to the TV station."

When questioned about music on television, 46 percent of the artists thought local music was played on TV several times a week, 27 percent believed daily, and nearly 20 percent, only once a week or less.

Over 40 percent (11 artists) said they got their music on TV by taking the record to the station. Seven said they did so by making a video and taking it to the station. A well known artist stated, "You have to pay the television stations (bribe them), the same as radio." One artist complained, "You have to have a video and money to make one, so if you are salt [broke], your music won't play on TV." Another said, "There is a shortage of locally-produced videotapes; therefore, local music tapes are in demand."

Three artists have used station access time. One said, "The Jamaica Broadcasting Station will record your group for free if they have free access and all rights to the footage, even for resale for profit to anyone, anywhere abroad." Another said, "If you wait until Carnival or festival time, they may film you for free and play it on TV."

Two interviewees observed that there was less local music on TV now than there used to be. An artist observed, "There used to be a TV series 'Where It's At' that ended in 1984. It was free." Another said, "I've done jazz with Hibbert in the 70s when they used to play a lot of reggae and jazzy bands."

Two artists each got music on TV through contacts ("knowing someone") or by invitation, and one artist each did so through their promoter or manager, through bribes and payola, and by the station recruiting them to perform.

Piracy[2]

The Jamaican music industry has developed within the framework of a loose copyright system in which there are few legal barriers to restrict individuals from enriching themselves without making any creative input. Reggae star Judy Mowatt provided a historical perspective in a 1983 interview.[3] She noted that, in the past, most artists made money only from the Jamaican market. When their records were pirated or sold abroad by their producers, the artist did not benefit. However, because Jamaican singers and musicians increasingly travel internationally, it is easier to find out when music is being pirated. In the survey of 26 recording artists conducted in 1986, three of the artists gave examples of hearing that their music was published abroad, completely unknown to them until someone saw their records on the shelves in Canada, the U.S., or Britain.

Another aspect of piracy has been that some Jamaican singers rearrange and sing a "version" of a foreign tune and sell it locally. They get away with this because the Jamaican market is too small to really affect the sales of a big foreign hit. Only if the record is distributed abroad would Jamaicans have to adhere to international copyright law. According to Jamaican radio announcer and popular music columnist, Winston Barnes, there is a market for versions because records come into the country via sources other than local distributors. Radio stations, discos, and sound systems play the record and a market is created. But because no distributor has rights for the particular label, the record is not available, so pirating steps in (*Gleaner* and *Sunday Gleaner* columns, Jan.-May 1983).

Barnes explained that the pirate makes masters from a copy of the original recording, alters the label formation, or simply presses blank labelled records. Pirating is lucrative because there are no royalties to be paid. It could be overcome if distributors would move quickly to acquire distribution rights for small labels.

The most large-scale aspect of pirating in Jamaica is the underground market of private copying of current hits, which threatened the viability of the legitimate market in the 1980s. In Jamaica, pirating is big business. Almost all of the 170 record shops on the island are involved in pirating to such an extent that demand for 45s and LPs has decreased significantly since 1980.

In 1977, 35 presses produced 40,000-50,000 records. By 1986, 16 presses accounted for 7,000-8,000 records. This decrease in record production was accompanied by a simultaneous increase in illegal cassette duplication.

Edward Lee, managing director of Dynamic Sounds and strong advocate of an anti-piracy law, estimated in an interview in 1987, that the underground market was over a half million in U.S. dollars annually. Such a figure is reasonable in view of estimates that at least 100 record shops copy between 25 and 30 songs every day, and the cassettes are sold for a minimum of about U.S. $10. Lee's company, Dynamic Sounds, contributed several thousand dollars during the 1980s to assist in research on piracy and help the Jamaican Cultural Development Commission produce posters warning against pirating.

A survey conducted with the assistance of the International Federation of Phonogram and Videogram Producers (IFPI) revealed, among other things, that records are not usually sold in the town of Savanna-la-mar in the southwestern part of the island, because popular hits are immediately mass-produced on cassettes and sold over the counter. The 1980s were clearly open season for pirating in Jamaica.

Harry Johnson, manager of Harry J's Recording Studio and Sunset Records Manufacturing Limited, stated in a 1987 interview, "As soon as we make a hit record, everybody has it. There are a lot of people with machines who just tape the records on blank tape and sell." There is enough evidence to substantiate this claim, and the concern from Neville Lee, manager of Sonic Sounds, which controls about 40 percent of local sales, is that both compact discs (CDs) and cassettes will very soon dominate the industry, making the present process of pressing vinyl obsolete.

Charles Simms, managing director of WKS Records and treasurer of the Jamaica Federation of Musicians, sees the problem as having international implications, since many national phonogram associations are trying to grapple with what has become a serious issue by means of applying international conventions as well as lobbying governments to strengthen national legislation. In Africa, Bob Marley is the most-pirated Jamaican artist, along with Peter Tosh, Jimmy Cliff, and Eric Donaldson.

On the international scene, according to the IFPI newsletter (June-July 1986; Aug.-Sept. 1986; Mar.-Apr. 1987), IFPI officials have the agreement of the Hong Kong Customs and Excise Department for close cooperation on anti-piracy matters. Nigeria recently fined a tape producer U.S. $75,000 for pirating music performed by Marvin Gaye, "Kool and the Gang," "Black Uhuru," and Rita Marley. Liberia is now drafting a new copyright law to combat a thriving underground market on the west African coast.

Many Jamaican producers and artists expressed the view that a copyright law similar to that of Trinidad & Tobago would effectively avert the rapid deterioration of the legitimate market. Trinidad & Tobago recently passed an anti-piracy act which protects local musicians from illegal taping of their songs without adequate remuneration. In addition, a new copyright law has also been passed. It grants producers of phonograms the right to authorize the reproduction and distribution of their phonograms and the right to receive an equitable remuneration for their broadcasting and public performance. This remuneration is to be shared equally with performers. Performers have the exclusive right to authorize the recording, broadcasting, and communication to the public of their performances, including communication by cable (IFPI 1986).

Trinidad's bold move to protect local musicians from the underground market attracted the interest of Jamaican producers and artists. In 1985, legal experts from Trinidad met with the Jamaican Federation of Musicians and representatives from Dynamic Sounds, among others, and shared information on certain aspects of a comprehensive copyright law. Record company managing director Simms sees the answer in the imposition of a levy. He feels that "whenever people bring in blank cassettes, they (government) should levy them a certain amount of money and give it back to the performing rights body or to the music union so that some form of benefit can be given to our members."

Copyright

Contracts and Copyright

Eighteen of the 26 musicians interviewed had made recordings, but only three of them had a formal contract with a recording company. Six said they had no formal contract and others had informal agreements, many of which turned out badly, as illustrated by the case studies above. One artist described his arrangement as follows:

We were paid a little weekly salary and had a verbal agreement to get royalties for records. One record made 'Cashbox'-240,000 copies sold—and they offered us nothing at all. When we went to Federal Record Company, they said they couldn't afford the rhythm section anymore. I became so frustrated that I packed up and left and have only been in a studio once since then.

Another artist said, "Ripoffs happen all the time, even Bob Marley's arranger/keyboard man is still struggling; he was treated badly by Bob and turned to coke."

Internationally-known reggae star, Marcia Griffiths, said she had only a verbal agreement with her producer, and that she hadn't used a lawyer because she "doesn't trust lawyers." In fact, only one musician said he/she had used a lawyer. Over half of the artists had never used a lawyer in production, and the remainder had not produced a record or did not answer. However, it is probably safe to assume that, although most musicians did not use a lawyer as individuals, they may have been members of bands which used a lawyer on behalf of all members.

Table 2

Copyright Ownership for Recordings or Tapes of Jamaican Musicians (N=18)

Ownership	No.	%
No copyright	4	22
Self or group on recording	7	39
Producer	2	11
Other	4	22
Don't know	1	6

Table 2 records the responses of the 18 musicians concerning ownership of the copyright to their recording or tape. One did not know who owned the copyright; 22 percent or four musicians said they had no copyright; nearly 40 percent or seven said they or the group on the recording owned it; and two artists said their producer owned it. Four artists described other arrangements: one artist owned it jointly with the producer; in another case, copyright was owned by the distributor/ producer; another artist said he and others had copyright, and one described the following "copyright" process:

I carry the tape to the Post Office and they stamp it and this proves it was written on such and such a date.

National and Regional Copyright Picture

There is probably no other national music industry which is so extensive and vibrant but has so little legislation to protect the people involved. In the words of Jamaican lawyer Lloyd Stanbury, in a 1986 letter to the editor: "Jamaican record producers are probably the only producers in the world who think that by merely spending their money, they become entitled to copyright in the songs composed by artists with whom they work." According to popular music columnist, Howard McGowan, "producers are getting into the business to get rich, not because they love the music or have a flair for it" (*Sunday Gleaner*, Sept. 21, 1986).

In our survey of 26 recording artists, most of the experienced ones said that the greatest need of Jamaica's authors, composers, and performers was for new copyright legislation. Jamaica's only copyright legislation is an archaic 1911 Copyright Act modelled on that of Great Britain. The UK Copyright Act of 1911 extends to several countries in the Commonwealth, not yet signatories to international conventions dealing with protection, remuneration, and infringement of artistic property. However, this act provides only very limited protection.

Further, Jamaica is not signatory to any international copyright convention, neither the Berne Convention of 1886 nor the Universal Copyright Convention of 1952, both of which were revised at Paris in 1971. This means that Jamaican works are usually not protected in other countries.

The UK Copyright Act was amended in 1956 to reflect technological advances. By 1974, the Jamaican government established a copyright committee which made several recommendations based primarily on the amended UK Act of 1956.[4]

After much agitation by local musicians and those within the industry, the government promulgated a Jamaican Copyright Act of 1977, which never became law, because the necessary administrative infrastructure was not properly organized to deal with important matters of optional registration, training, and policing international conventions. Tavares-Finson and Pereira highlight two other factors which stalled the act from becoming law.

First, a unit within the region's economic association, the Caribbean Community (CARICOM), urged the Jamaican government to proceed cautiously while re-examining the 1977 act, in light of modern means of communication and production. Second, strong dissatisfaction within the industry indicated that the act would not provide the type and level of protection producers and artists anticipated.

There was an attempt in 1973 to form a Caribbean Copyright Organization. Headed by one of Jamaica's leading artists, Bob Andy, with music publisher Ted Powder as Deputy, the CCO had noble ideals of providing a mechanism to repatriate copyright property, as well as protect economic rights of Caribbean artists. However, the organization never got off the ground, mainly because of unresolved copyright legislation at national levels. In addition, legal complexities associated with international copyright were beyond the limited resources of the CCO.

Delay in enforcing effective copyright legislation in Jamaica has also to do with reciprocity and proper registration of artistic composition. An extension of proper registration would be securing a comprehensive act which covers neighboring right—a cluster of rights which protect producers and artists from copyright infringement beyond their original compositions, e.g. performance of material by other artists at concerts, in films, and on television.

Reciprocity means Jamaica fulfills its obligations in respect of payment for overseas copyright works played on radio and television. Participating in any of the international conventions would guarantee locally-copyrighted material getting full remuneration locally and internationally. However, Jamaica's low exchange rate, resulting from severe devaluation during the 1980s, would cause undue difficulty for the electronic media to make necessary payments to ASCAP and BMI.

International conventions guarantee protection against unlawful duplication or performance of artistic works, and Table 3 lists the international conventions to which Caribbean countries have been signatories. Jamaica has not signed any of them.

Table 4 lists existing laws and conventions which govern copyright in English-speaking Caribbean countries.

In the absence of a copyright law which speaks to serious inequities within the industry, Jamaica contributes to England's Performing Rights Society (PRS), through a local office in Kingston. For over 50 years, Jamaica has had an agency of the PRS which seeks to collect performing right royalties for its members. Under existing copyright laws in Jamaica, a person who causes the performance or reperformance of a copyrighted work is liable to the copyright owners. According to attorney Harold Brady (*Sunday Gleaner*, Jan. 4, 1987), from time to time, the PRS has, acting on behalf of copyright owners in the music industry, taken successful action in the Jamaican courts to see that these rights are enforced.

Payments to the PRS are for performers only, not for producers or writers, and artists with foreign hits tend to be paid larger amounts than artists with hits in Jamaica.

Both radio stations pay an agreed sum for mechanical rights based on the frequency with which each artist receives airplay. In 1972, mechanical rights were three cents per play. The cost in the mid-1980s was ten cents for each time a record was played. Thus, every time the stations play a recording, they are expected to keep records which will facilitate payments of annual performers' fees.

In addition, Britain's Mechanical Copyright Protection Society (MCPS) licenses the recording and re-recording of many musical works in the United Kingdom, the Commonwealth, and the Republic of Ireland. It also seeks to collect royalties on the sales of recordings. A figure of 6 1/4 percent is authorized by the 1965 Copyright Act in England and operates when the parties are members of the England-based society. However, Jamaica is still governed by the 1911 Copyright Act, Section 19 (3) of which provides for only 5 percent on the ordinary retail selling price. Jamaica did not increase its rate to 6 1/4 percent as did Britain.

Furthermore, Jamaican lawyer Gayle Nelson has observed that, by current practice, Jamaican authors and composers usually receive less than five percent (*Sunday Gleaner* Nov. 17, 1985). In the early 1970s, when records were sold at $1 each, the producers paid 5 percent. However, as the price of records increased, the producers have not maintained the 5 percent royalty. In addition to that, it became common practice for

Table 3

International Conventions and Caribbean Territories

Country	Date of Entry		Country	Date of Entry
International Union for the Protection of Literary and Artistic Works (Berne, 1886)			Universal Copyright Convention (Geneva, 1952)	
Bahamas	10 July 1973		Bahamas	27 Dec. 1976
Barbados	30 July 1983		Barbados	18 June 1983
Suriname	23 Feb. 1977		Belize	1 Dec. 1982
			Cuba	18 June 1957
			Haiti	16 Sept. 1955
Convention for the Protection of Performers, Producers of Phonograms and Broadcasting Organizations (Rome Convention, 1961)			Convention for the Protection of Producers of Phonograms against Un-authorized Duplication of their Phonograms (Geneva, 1971)	
Barbados	18 June 1973		Barbados	29 July 1985

Source: International Conventions & Copyright, IFPI, 1986

the producer to record a "version" of the song on the flip side of the work, and then pay the writer only 2 1/2 percent, despite the fact that the version is a plagiarism of the music on the number one side. The producer keeps the two and one half percent for the flip side, usually laying claim to ownership thereof.

The same lawyer notes that problems experienced by recording artists as a result of the lack of up-to-date copyright legislation are created by both fellow authors, composers, and performers and by handlers of their work (whether companies or individuals). Nelson describes those who appropriate other people's material for their own use as plagiarists, and according to both Nelson and many of the recording artists interviewed, the plagiarist in Jamaica is often the producer. In Nelson's words,

The 'producer' has the rhythm track of the original work which he tends to regard, quite wrongly as his property although he properly owns the tape. He might employ someone to add to the original work, or he may use a 'mixer' (a studio engineer) to change the music. Then, he will foist on the public what he represents to be an altogether new 'sound.'

Table 4

Copyright Legislation in the Caribbean

Country	Legislation	Duration of Protection	Membership of Conventions
Bahamas	UK Copyright Act 1956	50 years from publication	Berne, UCC
Barbados	Copyright Act 1981	20 years from making or publication	Berne, UCC, Rome, Phonograms
Belize	Copyright Act 1956	50 years from publication	UCC
Grenada	UK Copyright Act 1956	50 years from publication	
Guyana	UK Copyright Act 1956	50 years from publication	
Jamaica*	UK Copyright Act 1911	50 years from making of plate	
T & T**	Copyright Act 1985	50 years from making of plate or publication	
Montserrat	UK Copyright Act 1956	50 years from publication	Berne, UCC, Phonograms
Cayman Is.	UK Copyright Act 1956	50 years from publication	Phonograms
St. Lucia	UK Copyright Act 1956	50 years from publication	Phonograms

Source: International Conventions & Copyright, IFPI, 1986
*Copyright Act amended in 1977 but not into law.
**Trinidad and Tobago passed a new copyright law in 1985.

In a June 1987 interview, Harry Johnson, owner and producer of Harry J's Recording Studio and Sunset Record Manufacturing Limited, felt strongly that "if we had a copyright law, we could publish here, and we could demand that JBC and RJR pay a certain amount of money to play songs. Right now is only the PRS [Performing Rights Society; see above]....The writers and composers are not getting any-thing....The composers should be getting compensation."[5]

The anger of Jamaican recording artists with this and other problems in the system was captured in the words of a musician who asked to remain anonymous:

Some of the people at the head are making a lot of bread from the system. If a new copyright law is enforced, they wouldn't be able to take other people's material as they do now and use it. They aren't willing to take the risk of having a new copyright law because they would lose.

It is painful to see artists, who live for their music, hurt both psychologically and financially by the recording industry system. Some of the problems in marketing their talents could have been averted if they were more sophisticated and less trusting, but their environment does not encourage this. Change is long overdue in a system which is discouraging the talent and killing the spirit even of artists who have proved their worth in the international market.

Chapter Six
On Interpreting Popular Music:
Zouk in the West Indies

Jocelyne Guilbault

One of the dominant features of life in most Caribbean communities is the people's continuing reliance on music to help them perform the most mundane chores or to celebrate the most special events. This means that there is a great deal of social value placed on popular music. Musical value judgments constitute such a social force in the West Indies that no one in power can ignore the impact music has on the way people make political decisions. As Everold N. Hosein stated after a survey in St. Lucia (1975, p. 17), the fact that most people find music the most important criterion in determining what is their favorite radio station has important implications for using radio-music-in communication strategies for planned development changes.

The importance and usefulness of music means that the most popular music heard on radio is in a key position not only to reveal what people are, but also to help them establish a sense of identity and to clarify ideals and motivations. As the British sociologist and rock music critic Simon Frith (1987, pp. 144-48) observed: 1. pop music sets up a narrative structure: it sets up star personalities, situates the listener, and puts into play patterns of identity and opposition; 2. the specific form of the musical genre affects the relative intensity of the listener's experience, and 3. each musical genre sets the notion of "truth" for its listeners. Popular music, Frith concluded, has ultimately a role of placement. "What pop can do is put into play a sense of identity that may or may not fit the way we are placed by other social forces" (1987, p. 149). It is specifically for this last reason that we need to examine the strategies and constraints that play a decisive role in determining the impact popular music has on individuals. Whether, as Frith suggested, "we want to value most highly that music...which has some sort of collective, disruptive cultural effect" (1987, p. 149) should be indeed a prime concern for anyone interested in understanding better how people, by adhering to, or opposing themselves against, the music presented to them, are led to conceive and perceive the world.

A prime example is *zouk*, a Caribbean popular genre that has been made famous by the group called Kassav. Its members, mainly composed of Guadeloupeans and Martiniquais who now live in Paris, have recorded over twenty albums during the past five years and have already been awarded several gold records. Their music is popular in Europe and has even reached the coast of Africa, where their phenomenal success is compared with that of the Beatles. Even though the achievements of Kassav may seem spectacular abroad, their popularity in the Windward Islands has reached staggering proportions. Several groups have recently been formed and perform strictly *zouk* music.[1] Twenty-four hours a day, radio stations play *zouk* music; TV channels regularly devote entire programs to it and present daily ten-to twenty-minute videos that introduce new releases. Discotheques that are identified as the "hot" spots play *zouk* at full volume all night.

Two main questions need to be addressed: 1. How do people make value judgements about music and how do such value judgments articulate the listening experiences involved (Frith 1987: 134). Put in more practical terms, how can the popular music called *zouk* generate a homegrown feeling for the most immediate audience for this music—that is, the inhabitants of Martinique, Guadeloupe, Dominica, and St. Lucia—whereas, say, reggae, in spite of its continued popularity in the islands, is still considered foreign music?[2] 2. Does, or can, *zouk* play a role in the regional integration of the Creole-speaking islands and if so, at what levels?[3] This last question, posed in 1981 by Yves Renard of the Caribbean Conservation Association, is perhaps more than ever an issue today. This is a dynamic period in the cultural and political history of Creole-speaking peoples, one in which the necessity of defining the Creole identity is becoming more and more urgent, in keeping with the major changes that will occur with the coming in 1992 of the "Acte Unique Européen" (Farrugia, Pépin et al ·1987)[4], and the ongoing preparations of the member countries of the Organization of the Eastern Caribbean States (OECS) to form a political federation (DaBreo 1988; Demas 1988).

In an attempt to answer these questions, this paper is divided into three sections.[5] The first introduces the key elements of the social and political settings, plus the soundscapes[6], of Martinique, Guadeloupe, St. Lucia, and Dominica that predispose people to make certain value judgements. The second section focuses on the making of *zouk* music to highlight how the composers create their music (consciously in some instances, non-consciously in others) to connect with the various social, political, and musical environments. The third section describes the relative impact this music has on people, by examining how it competes and compares with other types of popular music accessible on the islands, and how, as a social force, it fits in with other local social forces.

Social and Political Setting and Soundscape

Guadeloupe and Martinique are both French-and Creole-speaking countries that are politically, economically, and socially tied to France as departments. Although the two islands have enjoyed an average income far superior to that of any neighboring state, they have, however, felt very uneasy with French administration and law that superimpose ways of thinking and doing that do not meet their own needs and philosophies. Over time, the political dependency of Guadeloupe and Martinique has led the islanders to question their cultural identity. At times, what is defined by many Antillean writers as a "deep malaise," has had a paralyzing effect on artists and has brought creative production to a halt. At other times, this intellectual and emotional insecurity has incited several Antilleans to action, turning back to their folk traditions for inspiration in order to develop forms of expression that could help reassert their own identity. That is what the Kassav group has done.

Dominica and St. Lucia, former British colonies, are both English-and Creole-speaking islands that acquired political independence only in 1978 and 1979, respectively. Unlike the French—speaking islanders, Dominicans and St. Lucians are confronted less with questions of cultural identity than they are with problems of resources. The economies of both islands are such that, in most instances, artists have to leave home to find work. Those who do stay are faced with earning their living by working for the ministry of culture, where there is very little time to do creative work, or for commercial enterprises such as hotels, where creativity is rarely encouraged. Even when they have exceptional talent, artists do not have enough money to get their work adequately produced and promoted to reach a wide audience and be financially successful. As a result, these two islands have become great consumers of foreign products. How *zouk* music produced in the French departments is not considered foreign in St. Lucia and Dominica will be explained in the following pages.

Musical aesthetics are motivated or cultivated, not only by people's political and social surroundings, but also very much by their soundscapes. Listeners quickly assimilate familiar sounds into a series of associations that become part of their total experience. To assess the soundscape of a region and to examine its various meanings for the listeners in that region is, in fact, a prerequisite to understanding how a given music achieves its impact on the population.

The experience of music by Creole-speakers is affected by the following three powerful factors that help form their soundscape: mass media, migration patterns, and folk traditions.

The Mass Media

It is by now a truism that the overall selection of broadcast music influences the relative popularity of each musical genre. How is the selection made? As a result of programming policies, government legislation? Who supplies the recordings to the radio stations? What is the role of the broadcaster in the choice of music played on the air?

In St. Lucia, Dominica, Guadeloupe, and Martinique, there is a policy regulating the spoken content of radio programming, but there is none for the selection of music played on the program, that being totally left to the discretion of disc jockeys. The disc jockeys, who most of the time have learned the trade on the spot, follow their musical intuition and taste. Only recently, have telephone call-in shows allowed them to gauge musical tastes directly from listeners. Before the advent of call-in shows, disc jockeys picked up information by attending popular fêtes and listening to friends' comments on music. At times, as in Dominica, vans provided by radio stations circulated throughout the country to do programs on the spot. During these sessions, interviewers heard people's comments on the music. To this day, there is no other organization that can provide a profile of Dominicans' musical tastes and indicate the relative degree of popularity of specific musicians or musical genres.[7] Musical intuition and the availability of records are, in fact, at the heart of the decision—making process that determines what goes on the air.

In poor countries, such as St. Lucia and Dominica, the limitations on what a disc jockey can play are often imposed by external, economic constraints. The situation is more severe in Dominica, where records are no longer given free to radio stations, and Radio Dominica, for some time, has not supplied a budget big enough to keep up to date with new releases. For each broadcast, disc jockeys have to borrow, from friends' collections, the records they want to—and, indeed, must—play to maintain their personal popularity as disc jockeys. There is no weekend chart, say, of the "top 40," since these albums, borrowed during the week, are most often not available during the weekends.

In Guadeloupe and Martinique, there is no shortage of records, thanks to the French economic system and several zouk producers who live on the islands and send free copies to radio stations. However, in some instances, there are political constraints. Out of the rather large number of private radio stations[8] for the relatively small population of the French islands—29 radio stations for a population of 320,000 in Guadeloupe and 36 for a population of 360,000 in Martinique[9]—we are told that no more than five stations in each island reach a wide audience. These stations are, for the most part, each associated with a political party, which may or may not have a direct impact on the disc jockeys' selections of music. Certain separatist stations refuse to play anything other than traditional or politically-oriented music. Other stations have more liberal musical choices and, as in St. Lucia and Dominica, allow disc jockeys to be entirely responsible for the selection.

Apart from economic restraints which, as we have seen, have not yet prevented disc jockeys from finding the records they want to play, the music heard on the Creole-language radio stations in general reflects, as noted earlier, the disc jockeys' musical intuition.

Migration Patterns

Musical intuition reflects higher education which, within the political and economic systems of the four Creole-speaking islands, implies emigration. For the two former British colonies, higher education means going to Great Britain, the United States, Jamaica, Trinidad, and-for a few-Barbados. Most of the disc jockeys interviewed for this study had lived for three years or more in one of these places. Since there is little contact in these countries with Spanish or African music, none is played on the air, though the U.S. mass media have had a tremendous impact. Disc jockeys' habits, values, and models are marked by their experience abroad, and hence their taste for American music, reggae, calypso (and soca)[10] reflects it.

Disc jockeys' habits, values, and models are also marked by the continual movement within the region of the population at large. Apart from cultivating relations with the more obvious trade centers—such as Barbados, Trinidad, and Jamaica-St. Lucians and Dominicans have maintained a strong network of trade with Martinique and Guadeloupe, respectively, since the beginning of colonization.[11] The importing of goods has also meant the importing of music. Today, for example, two young businessmen from Dominica go to Guadeloupe, regularly each month, to buy records for their record shop. Several Dominicans have said these these two men alone have played a major role in promoting *zouk* on the island by making it available to radio stations, discotheques, and mobile discos. Touring groups over the years have also had an impact on the musical taste of disc jockeys, as well as the general population of the islands. The group Kassav's two visits to St. Lucia (in 1985 and 1986) helped the group to present itself more effectively and advertise its music. Kassav was already popular on the island, but after these visits, its popularity reached a peak on the local radio stations.

In Guadeloupe and Martinique, as in St. Lucia and Dominica, higher education implies leaving home. The usual destination is France, where the multi-ethnic population allows one to cultivate many tastes and meet many groups. The Antilleans are spontaneously attracted to African music and find it readily available among the many French-speaking African groups living in Paris. This interaction among Guadeloupeans, Martiniquais, and Africans, developed in France, has had a continuing influence back home through the efforts of a few disc jockeys who have become true afficionados of African music.

The blossoming of Latin music—from Cuba, Argentina, and Brazil—in the two French islands[12] comes less from migration than from the international fame of Latin music in the 1940s and 1950s and the access to it by medium-wave radios. By the mid-1960s, the popularity of Latin music was reinforced by Puerto Rican groups touring in the French island departments. The Puerto Ricans were later followed by groups from Santo Domingo (1978) and Cuba (1980). Even though Latin music is not as popular as it used to be in the French departments, it is still very much enjoyed, particularly by people over thirty-five years of age, and promoted locally by powerful artistic personalities.

Like Latin music, calypso (later soca) and reggae have entered the musical scene of Guadeloupe and Martinique via Europe, North America, and the Caribbean, where they acquired international fame. Calypso reached its peak of popularity between 1960 and 1965 when well-known artists, such as "Mighty Sparrow," visited the islands. After this period, calypso has been heard only occasionally. Reggae, too, enjoyed great popularity but only for a short time between the late 1970s and early 1980s when it came to be treated as a marginal music form.

In the French departments, *zouk* music belongs to an entirely different category; it is a homegrown product, part of the musical history and experience of the people. If today it is recognized as homegrown, it is nevertheless related to the immigration history of the islands, as it was greatly influenced by the dance rhythm called *cadence* brought over by Haitians[13].

Zouk also features other musical ingredients, some taken directly from Guadeloupean and Martiniquais musical folk traditions—as, for example, the *mizik vidé* (carnival music)—and others that come from the blend of their unique musical experience and the integration of American, Latin, and African music. *Zouk* has been very much a natural outcome of the particular soundscape of these French departments.

Folk Traditions

The Caribbean experience of popular music is shaped not only by the musical content of mass media and the deep effects of migration patterns, but also by what is at the root of the aesthetic sensibilities of the people—namely, folk traditions.

Folk traditions have perhaps been the strongest elements, along with the Creole language, that have contributed to the maintenance of special relations between Martinique, Guadeloupe, Dominica, and St. Lucia. The islands' history and development have followed a similar colonization pattern. The African, French, and English musical influences have developed in the region into families of musical genres that are easily recognizable today, in spite of the distinctive stylistic features that have evolved on each island.

The family of musical genres can be organized according to the following categories: 1. the *bélè* and *gwo ka* drum—accompanied song-dances; 2. the quadrille, with related ballroom dances and their typical instrumental accompaniment, and 3. carnival music and its musical ensembles. The outline is a crude representation of the rich diversity of the musical genres of each island, but the main goal is to describe the aesthetic qualities of these families that have so deeply marked the musical values and experience of the Creole-speaking peoples.[14]

The *bélè* and *gwo ka* drum-accompanied song-dances are normally enjoyed for their spectacular interactive playing, dancing, and singing. These songs are characterized by a call-and-response form, a close coordination between the dancers' steps and the rhythmic strokes of the drummer, and by an obvious, intense involvement of the lead singer, who sings constantly at full volume, with no vibrato, often exploiting the top of his or her vocal range. Active participation by everyone present in the dancing and singing is the key to a successful performance.

The quadrille and the related ballroom dances highlight another sort of musical excitement strongly linked with the colonial past. Quadrille performances have always been highly valued. Historically, demonstrations of knowledge about the choreography and social edge of the dance gave the dancers prestige and a share of the power associated with the European traditions. Musicians, too, were praised for mastering this sort of music which—everyone recognized—rested on a musical language with melodies, chords, and a bass line accompaniment rather different from the *bélè* and *gwo ka* song—dances.

Carnival music can theoretically include any music and instrument that will make people dance. Traditionally, percussive instruments of all sorts have marked the jump-up in the streets. Carnival music is characterized by lively melodies and a medium-fast marked beat, and it is played as loudly as possible. The focus of the singing, dancing, and playing of instruments is on the intensity of the act, on maximizing the effects.

To summarize the aesthetic values linked with the traditional musical scene:

1. Music rarely goes without singing, cannot go without dancing;

2. For a type of music to be "hot", it needs to be loud and intense;

3. The popularity of a musical genre is largely dependent on the way the music incites people to participate, and the more participants, the more successful the presentation is;

4. Musical performances are conceived as public entertainments and hence have to be spectacular, colorful, and well-timed;

5. Knowledge of the music of other groups and peoples is part of West Indian traditions, and versatility is highly valued;

6. A great sense of rhythmic timing, a convincing interpretation, and controlled rhythmic and melodic improvisation are associated with good and knowledgeable musicians.

These musical characteristics and the associations they arouse in the Caribbean definitely affect the way people experience music. To be aware of them, but, even more, to use these musical characteristics to make certain connections, as the musicians of Kassav have done so skillfully can be considered an integral part of that group's success.

To trace the network of the social, political, economic, and affective meanings associated with the many facets of popular music, one must first inquire about the socio-political, as well as the musical, background of the region that is, the effects of mass media, patterns of mobility, and folk traditions. Only then can one appreciate how much the form, content, and style of performance of a musical genre (such as *zouk*) draw from and build people's conceptions, perceptions, and patterns of consumption.

Narrative Structures of Zouk

How do the performers of *zouk* make up their own music and build their star image? Following is an examination of the *zouk* group that has been the most influential and the most popular, Kassav.[15]

As in any other musical genre—especially so-called popular music—the narrative structures of *zouk* refer not only to the music but also to the whole process of packaging. This includes the image (the personality) projected by the star, the language, tone of voice, gestures, pattern of identity (and opposition) put into play, and how the artist and the music performed situate the listener.

Unlike reggae artists who traditionally present themselves as non-conformists, as politicized and religious believers, *zouk* performers promote themselves as emancipated people who not only accept, but actually *reassert*, their cultural identity-that is, their multi-ethnic and musical crossbreed, their Creole language, their beliefs and customs. The "ideology" of the leading group, Kassav, is to reflect and promote a professional and cultural consciousness. The message of these *zouk*-makers is to believe in the "difference," to exhibit and exploit the plurality of their racial and musical backgrounds. *Zouk* performers, as has been noted by the linguist Félix Prudent of Martinique[16], have consciously chosen not to maintain a political stance, but instead to launch a cultural movement called by many artists, fans, and critics, the *mouvans zouk*. This movement fosters a new attitude and a particular lifestyle, of which Kassav is one of the clearest exponents.

The label *zouk*, strategically chosen by Kassav to identify the new form of Antillean music they play, is a Martiniquais word that refers to parties at which the greatest freedom of expression is allowed. By association with the term, *zouk* music has become the musical symbol of relief from normative social codes and individual autonomy.

In line with the label they chose, the group Kassav and its followers have opted to sing in the native tongue, Creole, as opposed to the two official languages in the islands, French and English. This choice, as will be explained later, has had a great impact on the Creole-speaking islands.

A choice of language can be made for political reasons and for the reaffirmation of one's cultural identity. It can become a marketing device to attract a particular audience or promote a particular area of the world. Kassav's choice of singing in Creole is linked to all of these reasons. From the several interviews published in magazines and newspapers, and in the author's personal meetings with their producers, press agents, and radio promoters, it is clear that the Kassav performers initially had their own reasons to sing in Creole. Living in Paris for over eight years, they have been confronted every day with the reminder that they are different, that they are *Antillais*. Singing in one's native tongue establishes one's identity.

At the same time, the members of Kassav also reflect the political situation back home. To sing in Creole has been as much a way to show solidarity with their compatriots in the French island departments, as it has been a marketing device to attract them and other Creole speakers to buy their records.

To hear popular tunes in Creole on the radio is indeed a special experience for Creole listeners. It not only evokes a feeling of home but it also reinforces an affective link with the Creole-speakers of other islands. This link is all the more understandable when it is recalled that, not long ago, it was forbidden to speak Creole in schoolyards and in homes that were striving for respectability. For the speakers of the language, Creole catches and embodies the full value of emotions that can be properly translated through its rhythm and the articulated sound.

Outside the Caribbean region, singing in Creole has helped Kassav to be identified quickly on the map. It has also incited other minorities to recognize and support the group, to whom they feel a bond because of similar political, economic, and social histories and because of current conditions. Whether Kassav has helped to promote tourism in the region or to create a special exotic appeal for the public at large has yet to be determined.

The song-texts produced by Kassav reflect linguistic sensitivity as much in the form as in the content. Desirous to appeal to a large audience and yet to use Creole in his songs, the leader of the Kassav group, Pierre-

Édouard Décimus, has eliminated certain Creole sounds, replacing them with others more assimilable to French ears. His interest in the phonetic aspect of song-texts has eventually led the members of the group to explore the natural rhythm and inflection of Creole to produce poetic texts that not only say things, but that agreeably sound as well.[17] This new attitude toward Creole (by using it openly and exploring its full potential as a language) goes hand in hand with Kassav's will to create texts that speak about Caribbean life. Members of the group refuse to sing pornographic songs, to talk only about love, or to recount stories that could not be understood by a wide audience. Instead, they focus on making the Antilles known by speaking about generic themes that evoke Antillean ways of life and social conditions, for example, by talking about their love for music (in the song "An ba la tè"), their respect for their ancestors (in "Pou zòt"), and their philosophy of life (in "Tout la rivyè"). One notable exception is their treatment of some love songs. One Kassav singer, unlike other members of the group, is famous for writing lyrics that contrast strongly with the Antillean tradition. Instead of projecting the usual macho image, he establishes a new kind of rapport between men and women; in his texts, women are respected and men are freer to speak the words of love. His lyrics are considered by many Antilleans of both sexes to be a true revolution in the song-text tradition of their countries.

Very early in the career of the group, several members of Kassav began to star individually or in pairs under their own names, but with the same Kassav musicians for accompaniment. This strategy, as the musical director of Kassav explained, was made for commercial reasons and aimed at creating a wider market. The impact has been much more than just monetary. The group has reached listeners in a profound and personal way; fans have been able to associate themselves closely with one star, while maintaining a connection with the group. Highly valued in West Indian societies, the image of the virile, tender, sentimental, energetic man, and the attractive female, are all represented by the group Kassav. For women, the female star has become a role model of success and emancipation.

These different personalities set up patterns both of identification and opposition; they provoke fans to react, to adopt certain behaviors, and to reject others. The *zouk* stars bring forward a heightened affirmation of the Creole identity by the use of the Creole language; the texts play with Caribbean imagery, and the music is directly linked with the Creole-speakers' soundscape. On the one hand, the *zouk* phenomenon has generated a new confidence in Creole-speakers to be able to "make it" and even excel in some sectors, as, for example, in music. On the other hand, Kassav, by reasserting its multi-ethnic background, has also encouraged fans to nurture the links they have with other cultural groups musically, to revamp their own performances, and politically and economically, to cherish this mark of solidarity.[18]

The image of emancipation projected by *zouk* performers owes much to *zouk* choreography. On stage, the performers execute carnival walking steps, and jump up, hands in the air, while their whole bodies accentuate the beat of the music. On a dance floor, however *zouk* is normally danced in closed-couple formation, in which partners are so close that, as the expression goes, *sé toufé yen yen* (not even a fly could pass between the couple without being squashed). *Zouk* music is associated with *wimé*, and with *manpa*, two qualificatives used in traditional music to refer to a "hot" (sexually charged) dance.

In 1986, in one of their concerts at the famous Zénith hall in Paris where over 8,000 people attended, Kassav performers began their show by saying:

ça va bien? *Mèsi pou zòt vini oswè-a. E cho—la, sé zòt, apwè, sé nou. Donk oswè-a, sé lawmòni...*

(Everything all right? Thank you for coming tonight. And this show, it's yours, and after, it's ours. So, tonight, it's harmony...)[19]

Kassav performers identify their listeners as a community of friends among whom racial and social differences are downplayed. The key word, as they said in their show at the Zénith, is "harmony." The crowd at their concert becomes part of the group and part of the show by being encouraged to answer back, make physical gestures, such as *lévé lanmen* (raise your hand) and *soté, soté* (jump up, jump up). The song-leader develops a warm interaction with the crowd and treats everyone present as a member of the same family.

Forms and Styles of Popular Music

The ingredients of popular music have traditionally been dismissed from serious musicological studies because of their so-called simplicity. However, some forms and particular singing styles seem to correspond to special aesthetic values for specific groups of people by raising great admiration and participation. How does the choice of musical elements influence the intensity of musical experience? This question, asked by Simon Frith (1987, pp. 144-46), will serve to guide this examination of *zouk* music.

The musical form of *zouk* songs is based on the typical West Indian tradition of alternating a song-leader with a chorus. The song-leader sings two or more melodies and the chorus sings a corresponding number of musical sections. Brass sections, most of the time in unison like most choirs in traditional West Indian music,[20] make up the bridges between sections, play short instrumental periods, and provide punchy lines in between vocals. A range of percussive instruments play against the drum set, which, in turn, is a tributary of the bass line. The whole arrangement is based on interactive playing to the point where many *zouk* songs are very difficult to sing without the musical accompaniment.[21]

Zouk arrangements, in order for the music to be complete and to come alive, call for a smooth collaboration of the musicians and full participation of the crowd. The intensity of a *zouk* experience comes from this full-scale interaction and the feeling that everyone is as much a part of the song as a possessor of it.[22] This highly interactive form of song has a special resonance in the Caribbean. Packaged with the most modern instruments, *zouk* songs are nevertheless connected to Creole song traditions. Several traditional songs are indeed based on interactive patterns. For example, the *bèlè* songs from Martinique, the *mizik gwo ka* from Guadeloupe, the *koutoumba* songs from St. Lucia, and the *lapo kabwit* from Dominica all rely on multi-parts to be performed. This principle of making music is dear to Creole-speakers and even preferred over soloists accompanied by musical instruments. The musical form of *zouk* has thus a direct impact on Creole-speakers by making a connection with their musical experience and tastes.

Singing style (verbal articulation, rhythmic vocal function, vocal inflection, and volume) also contributes to the impact of music on people. *Zouk* performers employ the familiar Caribbean duple, rather than triple, division for the lyrics, and sing the words in a syllabic fashion, as in most Caribbean songs. Also typical of the Creole singing style, the voices take on a rhythmic function by using the scat singing technique—that is, by substituting for the words of a song, improvised nonsense syllables to increase the percussive and rhythmic effect. The intensity of the singers is particularly noticeable through the sustained loudness of voice and the vocal inflection, which is energetic, dynamic, and percussive. All these qualities, held in high esteem in traditional Creole music performances, serve to heighten participation and are used to elicit crowd response.

There are rhythmic patterns in a musical culture that no one can resist. Associated with specific images, times, and places, they belong to the soundscape, to the music with which one grew up. To rely on these motifs is a sure way to reach an audience.

The musicians of Kassav are very conscious of these powerful rhythmic patterns. They rely heavily on them to create a mood and to elicit participation in order to make their listeners live a particular experience at a particular intensity.[23] An example of these rhythms is the carnival rhythmic call on a single note, to which the crowd unmistakably answers " *yè, yè*" as the key expression to show its support of the rally. This rhythm is not heard as make-believe carnival, it *becomes* carnival.

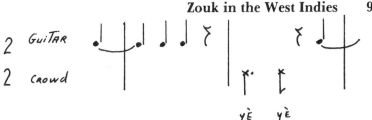

Popular Music and the Notion of "Truth" or Reality

This brings us to the next point. Pop music sets out a particular reality. The image the star personalities project, the acts they perform, the tone of voice they use, the language they choose, the relation they cultivate with the public, the concert experience they bring, all these incite fans to react. In reacting, they adopt specific attitudes and develop various ideas about their identity and ways to apprehend the world, in relation to other star images, performed acts, tones of voice, other spoken languages, other types of interaction with the public, and other lived experiences. The success of pop music, not surprisingly, is often judged by its ideological effects. In this case, the question is: how is *zouk* perceived and compared with the other musical genres heard on the islands of Martinique, Guadeloupe, Dominica, and St. Lucia.

In the French islands, one can hear, apart from *zouk*, the Caribbean merengue, salsa, reggae, calypso (and soca), African *soukous*, American disco, traditional music of Martinique and Guadeloupe, and French music. Of the many possible responses to these types of music, that of the Guadeloupeans and Martiniquais is more or less the same. Even though the majority of the population does not understand the Spanish lyrics, merengue is still very popular, especially with rural people. Its fast rhythm constitutes the main attraction for them, while the overall effect of the music is said to be a symbol of joy.

Salsa is enjoyed mainly by intellectuals and people living in the urban centers of the French islands. Its choreography and rhythm, more elaborate than those of the merengue, particularly attract the very good dancers among these groups. Even though the texts of salsa are understood by many of its devotees, it is the overall musical arrangements that are found especially captivating. Salsa is considered to be equivalent to jazz. The genre is associated with refinement, and it is acknowledged as a potential source of prestige for those who can master the music and the choreography.

Calypso and soca were once very popular in the French islands, where many calypso artists toured. Today, it has no more meaning than mere carnival accompaniment. According to many observers, the arrangements have become too traditional and cannot compete with newer music. The English lyrics also prevent this music from reaching and maintaining a connection with the French islanders.

Reggae is strongly related to Rastas from Jamaica, to a foreign music with a foreign ideology. It is appreciated mostly by a minority of young people who understand English and who participate in their own way in the Rastafarian ideology; it is enjoyed by a few others who like to dance.

For the past two or three years, African music has achieved a growing popularity in the French islands.[24] The texts of the songs and personalities of the stars are little known to the larger public, but the music is greatly appreciated for dancing. Because it is executed with great freedom of movement, African music is considered as a "musique de defoulement," a way of releasing one's surplus energy.

American music knows only a moderate success in Martinique and Guadeloupe. It attracts young people and some intellectuals, but in general, is not much appreciated. At a private party, in fact, it is said that American music will be played to signal that the evening is over.

The traditional music of the French islands is played regularly on radio stations. In the context of the French departmental system, it is linked with politics and self-identity and is associated with the local scene.

Music from France is heard mostly on RFO, the government radio station of the two French departments. As a symbol of France, it is always received with reserve, as a form of cultural expression that still remains foreign to French Creole-speakers.

Zouk music is altogether different from any other broadcast music in the French West Indies. It is a music from home, sung in Creole, that has succeeded in reaching the international market. *Zouk* has thus become a symbol of success and the ideological leaven of the Creole identity and sensibility.

In St. Lucia and Dominica, *zouk* competes with American music, reggae, calypso (and soca).

American music, particularly country and western, and soul music, has been part of the Dominican and St. Lucian soundscapes for over thirty years. Country and western is extremely popular, especially with rural people who use it as their equivalent for a slow dance and even categorize it as traditional music. Both country and western and soul music are considered to be the best channels for expressing emotions. Country and western music, because of its strong association with themes of love and stories about "real" people, is actually used by many local religious groups.

Reggae music is characterized by passionate lyrics that denounce the economic oppression of the ruling white caste. In poor counties such as St. Lucia and Dominica, these messages have had a special resonance. However, because of its association with *ganja* (drug) and some unconventional behavior, the ideology of reggae has not been supported by the majority of the population in these islands, in spite of tremendous musical success in the 1970s and early 1980s.

Calypso (and later soca) has been part of the St. Lucian and Dominican soundscapes since the 1940s. Even more than traditional music, calypso, which has kept up with the times, is now at the center of the musical environment. Calypso (and soca) lyrics have had such an impact that complete linguistic expressions and inflections are now part of the people's vocabulary. The jump-up, the walking steps, and the hands in the air-the typical choreography of calypso-have become an instant reflex, performed at the sound of any dynamic music. The social comment that pervades the lyrics of calypso tunes has alerted the population to social and political problems and has helped develop a sense of critical thinking.

The tremendous popularity of calypso (and soca) in both Dominica and St. Lucia might partly explain why *zouk* has not had quite the steamroller effect it has had in the French island departments. Calypso (and soca), like *zouk*, are up-tempo music. However, unlike *zouk*, which, in general, does not make political and social comment, calypso (and soca) lyrics are famous for condemning injustices and commenting on epidemics and other destructive phenomena that plague the world. *Zouk*, for St. Lucians and Dominicans, is decidedly exhilarating; it is close to home by being sung in Creole and by being danced with traditional choreography. But there is no more to it than that, as is explained by their attitude to the *zouk* lyrics.

As Creole-speakers, Dominicans and St. Lucians understand the general ideas expressed by the *zouk* lyrics, but they rarely pick up, or try to pick up, the details of the songs. This is not only because they do not always understand the different accents and expressions of the Guadeloupeans and Martiniquais, but rather because, according to them, this is not where the message lies. The message of *zouk* for St. Lucians and Dominicans is to free oneself from tension, to live in harmony, and to "jump up."

The ideological effect of *zouk* music, pursued through a series of strategies, has reached the Creole-speakers. The degree to which it has, however, is largely dependent on the competing musical genres that are part of the soundscape of each island. The next question, therefore, is whether *zouk* evokes, and affirms, a sense of identity that fits (or does not fit) the way Creole-speakers find themselves situated in relation to other social forces.

Zouk as a Social Force and Its Fit with Other Social Forces

There are three key elements in the *zouk* Creole message: emancipation, social harmony, and cultural consciousness. Such themes would normally go along with times of political or social reform, or peace and free exchange. It is significant that *zouk* has become extremely popular precisely at a time when these slogans are for the most part negated by other social realities.

At present, the unemployment rate in the French island departments, as in Dominica and St. Lucia, has reached alarming proportions. More than 75 percent of the youth between the ages of 18 and 25 is unemployed. Because of this high unemployment, illegal emigrants from Dominica and St. Lucia are less than tolerated. Repeatedly, blatant racial discrimination confronts the different ethnic groups.

The political situation in Guadeloupe and Martinique is the subject of endless discussions and a source of great tension among various groups. The constant questioning by the Martiniquais about their identity periodically becomes a social malaise, a paralyzing force for people in all walks of life. Separatist parties in Guadeloupe have, on occasion, strongly protested some government decision, and at times this has led to social unrest in the entire population.

The tensions between Martiniquais and Guadeloupeans have not diminished over the years, and any talk about "harmony" between the islands will draw a smile. Not long ago, the writer was told that a group of Guadeloupean workers went on strike when they learned that a Martiniquais had been appointed head of their public institution.

The overwhelming exodus of Antillais to France has created a double source of alienation: a persistent uneasiness in their European milieu and, on their return home, a continual frustration.

In Dominica, the economic depression has severed many people's hopes of ever being able to improve their lot on the islands. Young people leave every year, with no expectation of returning.

In St. Lucia, the national income remains insufficient to support any significant industry, even though growing tourism has somewhat helped the economy. Unemployment, as in other islands, is extremely high for young people.

As can be seen, the images of emancipation, social harmony, and cultural consciousness that *zouk* projects do not reflect the desolate economic situation of the islands nor the pronounced animosity between various groups in the region. However, in contrast with (or reaction against?) this stark picture, there are numerous signs-connected with the slogans of *zouk*—that reflect a new movement toward mobilizing resources, setting up a skill-exchange network, and putting artistic talents at the service of the public.

Over the past five years in St. Lucia and Dominica, great efforts have been made to set up non-government organizations to promote the development of small enterprises, for example, National Research Development Foundation in St. Lucia and Small Project Association Team in Dominica. Numerous workshops uniting people from

Guadeloupe, Martinique, St. Lucia, and Dominica have been organized to compare and trade experiences. Plays have been written as vehicles for popular education in rural areas and video programs have been produced to teach workers about new fishing, farming, and manufacturing techniques and environmental issues. As part of the same movement, many arts groups have been striving to find new means of expression that would achieve balance between the local and the international, by not denying, but affirming, their musical traditions and linking them with the present. As the economies of the islands have worsened over the past few years, a quiet but active underground network has been formed to fight the psychological depression that has started to grow among young and old people alike.

In the French islands, there is, paradoxically, along with the ethnic tensions, a new interest, in next-door neighbors St. Lucia and Dominica. As the economic situation has deteriorated, a sense of solidarity between the islands has developed. For example, instead of always going to Europe or Venezuela for their vacations, the French islanders have now begun to travel more within the region, as is shown by the noticeable increase of tourism from the French islands to St. Lucia. In 1982, the St. Lucia Tourist Statistics Office recorded 4,545 French visitor; five years later, the number reached 7,795. No other area has shown a similar increase in number of visitors to St. Lucia.[25] In addition, several associations from Guadeloupe and Martinique have organized group exchanges with their counterparts in St. Lucia and Dominica.

It can be seen that *zouk* has undeniably had a collective cultural effect. This is confirmed by the spectacular record sales, the formation of many *zouk* groups, the talk shows organized to discuss the phenomenon, the influence of *zouk* on many other musical genres, such as soca and *zouk*—soca. But how it has been disruptive is another question.

In St. Lucia and Dominica, the popularity of *zouk* can be seen as disruptive insofar as it has raised, for the calypso organization, the problem of whether *zouk* music should enter the calypso road march competition. Ideologically speaking *zouk* has had the positive effect of encouraging some urban people to return to their Creole language which, for a long time, had been downplayed. Through its popularity, *zouk* has reinforced a feeling of solidarity among the islands' Creole-speakers.

It is in Guadeloupe and Martinique that *zouk* has perhaps had the more collective, disruptive cultural effect. *Zouk* has run counter to many established institutions. For example, it has opposed the Haitian recording industry dominant for over twenty years in the French-speaking islands, as well as the French official language; it has projected a conciliatory image, opposing the division between local political factions and the continued division between Guadeloupe and Martinique; and it has turned its back on the French islanders' confusion and constant self-questioning about their identity, and has instead affirmed the *Antillanité* of the people. The *zouk* message have come across not only in lyrics but perhaps even more forcefully in the entire packaging process. As Derek Walcott wrote, "...[West Indian art] is so visibly, physically self-expressive" (1973, pp. 305-06). *Zouk* has effectively exploited precisely this West Indian characteristic of intense physical experience in sound, beat, and choreography to counteract other realities. And it is interesting that in the process, it has alleviated the economic situation at least in one sector-the record industry-by injecting new life, developing new prospects, and opening doors for young artists.

Zouk *as a Potential Factor in the Regional Integration of the Creole-Speaking Islands*

In 1974, in a speech on West Indian nationhood and Caribbean integration, the former secretary-general of the Caribbean community, William G. Demas, described the process of Caribbean integration as essentially not resting on economic factors, but rather on the successful promotion, primarily, of a sense of identity on the part of the people of the region. He then illustrated how identity is connected with development, on the one hand, and with unity, on the other. By identity, Demas meant, "the kind of identity that goes with self-confidence or rather that generates self-confidence, the kind of identity that generates a feeling of self-respect, self worth and inner dignity on the part of the people" (1974, p. 26). In another portion of his speech, he was more specific, quoting Naipaul's injunction, "identity springs from achievement."

If *zouk* has anything to do with regional integration, it is in its promotion of islanders' identity and with having achieved spectacular success at home and abroad. The main goal of the members of Kassav has been clear from the outset: to show the world they are Antillais and they can make a success of their art. By fulfilling their mission, they have given new confidence to young artists and producers. Before the advent of Kassav, no local sponsors would have placed their money on a local musical group. Today, local firms believe in local talent.

To sing in Creole, to rely on local rhythms, and to sing about typical West Indian behaviors and values as Kassav does (even though many people have criticized Kassav for not being local enough), all these have contributed to the reassertion of the *Antillanité* of the group's members and their compatriots.

When Demas (1974, p. 27) says that "the identity of a nation does not result merely from that nation producing a few gifted artists and writers" and that "a sense of identity of a people [can only] spring from achievement," he fails to recognize that artists can represent a role model of achievements at an individual and social level. From the success of

Kassav, Creole-speakers have understood very well that the only route to achievement lies through hardwork, discipline, the development of knowhow, and the introduction of creative innovations.

Caribbean identity and regional integration can be promoted by offering cultural alternatives to the foreign programming that invades the regional mass media. *Zouk* has helped the process of "decolonization" by putting local music into the top slot on radio. Furthermore, it has helped implant in some instances, and support in others, a process of indigenization rooted in the internal development of local cultural expression (see Paget 1983). The success of Kassav has indeed prompted many groups to reaffirm their Creole identity: 1. by taking on Creole names-after the fashion of the group "Kassav"—instead of English or Spanish names, as most groups did in the past;[26] 2. by singing in Creole instead of French, English, or Spanish; and 3. by rethinking their traditional music to find a local rhythm—as did Kassav with the Guadeloupean traditional *menndè*—that could be adapted and become a new music.

The ultimate challenge for Creole-speakers, however, remains to agree on the definition of the Creole identity, as suggested by Kassav. *Zouk* music has been provocative for many traditionalists, separatists, and other observers, because it uses a fusion of elements (apart form traditional motifs, one can sometimes hear in *zouk* the Haitian *cadence-rampa*, the American funk style, the African *soukous* riff on guitar, etc.) to revive and promote the Creole identity. By so doing, it raises in the minds of "purists" the old questions of how authentic, indigenous, or representative of the Creole-speaking countries this music is.

What Kassav has proposed is not only to accept, but to use to their full potential, the various influences that Creole-speakers have experienced musically. Translated to a broader level, Kassav has proposed recognition and celebration of the multi-ethnic background of Creole-speaking peoples. By presenting, with *zouk*, a fusion of various musics to reassert the Creole identity, the Kassav group has forced all of the islanders to come to terms with their own reality.

Acknowledgements

I am most grateful to the Social Sciences and Humanities Research Council of Canada for sponsoring this research. I want to express my heartfelt thanks to the many West Indian friends without whom this work could not have been done. I also wish to express my thanks to Line Grenier and François Tousignant for their helpful advice and criticism.

Chapter Seven
Local Music and Jamaican Politics:
The 1972 Elections

Gladstone Wilson

Introduction

Music as a part of the Jamaican political process dates from the epoch of slavery when slaves expressed their resentment through drumming, ring games, and ritualized folk traditions. These forms of communication were of high functional value in a predominantly oral setting.

Resistance to British colonialism manifested itself in two forms, namely political rebellion and retentions of indigenous traditions and popular culture. To hasten the end to slavery and the decolonizing process, several revolts were planned and executed by leaders of the black majority population. Sam Sharpe's slave revolt of 1831 and the 1865 Morant Bay rebellion were significant political acts which signalled the power of collective action by the disinherited.

Cultural resistance to external domination has been more subtle, enduring, and eclectic. In dance, poetry, drama, and music, absorption of some external influence has led to creolization. However, it is popular music that has had the greatest direct influence on Jamaican politics. So important has been this influence that political leaders either listen intently in order to reflect those expressions in public policy and pronouncements, or, in other cases use the music as part of general social protest against political opponents.

The clear potential of music in cultural patterns, and as a consequence, political thinking, was evidenced in the country's 1944 constitution.

When Universal Adult Suffrage was granted in 1944, a provision expressly barred the use of live bands from performing at political gatherings. It read, inter alia, "No person shall, for the purpose of promoting or procuring the election of any candidate, hire any band of music" (People's Act, 1944).

The law also pertained to musicians and artists. Contravention of this provision could have resulted in summary conviction.

Colonial authorities had an option of enforcing the 1911 *Night Noises Prevention Law* as a deterrent to the use of music in political agitation. Persons could be liable for prosecution if any singing or noise was audible beyond two chains after being asked to desist from making such sounds or noises (Law 31 of 1911).

P.J. Patterson, Q.C., chairman of the People's National Party, and the party's campaign manager for the 1972 elections, opines that the colonial masters feared music by live bands could have had an undue influence on voters. He added that, "And indeed, as a matter of history, that law remained on the statute books until we (the PNP) changed it, deliberately, in 1976" (Interview, Patterson, 1987).

While those who ran the colonial state viewed as dangerous the unchecked use of popular music in the electoral political "debate," a new generation of political activists utilized it in 1972 to channel serious social discontent.

This paper will demonstrate how social and political commentary in local music between 1968 and 1972 became a potent voice for lower status groups in economically-depressed areas of the country's capital, Kingston. As a result, the music helped to spawn an underclass solidarity on social and political issues.

The People's National Party (PNP)—then in opposition— channelled social discontent by utilizing indigenous popular music and leading local artists as part of the party's national campaign for state power. It was the only occasion in Jamaica's political history that local music was so integrated into a successful political contest.

Pre-1972: Socio-Political Crisis

Essentially, social tension and a rise in political activism provided fertile ground for the PNP's 1972 election campaign. Between 1962 and 1972, employment grew from 13 percent to 24 percent, particularly affecting youth and women. Girvan et al (1980, p. 115) states that the slums of Kingston, the main receptacle of rural-urban migration, were riddled with poor housing conditions, high unemployment, and wanton lack of social facilities. Prosperity and social deprivation stood in sharp relief to each other.

After independence in 1962, the racial/class harmony envisioned by many and captured in Jamaica's national motto "Out of Many, One People," was short-lived as racial tensions soon exacerbated social inequalities and class antagonisms ever-present in post-colonial societies. Prince Buster's "Black-Head Chinaman" spoke sharply of the economic preeminence of minority indentured East Indians and Chinese and migrant Lebanese groups, and of the denial to the majority of its proper place in the cultural, socio-economic ethos of society.

Perceptibly, Buster's song went to the heart of racial differences which later sparked race riots in 1965 and 1968. Thus began a powerful tradition in Jamaica—although well developed in Trinidad—in which social/political commentary became a regular feature of popular music.

Between 1967 and 1972, the ruling Jamaica Labour Party (JLP) became more repressive, harassing radical political activists, seizing passports, banning literature and songs with potent political messages. Dr. Walter Rodney, a Guyanese lecturer at the University of the West Indies, Mona, involved in radical politics, was refused entry after returning from a Black Writers' conference in Canada. In addition, the Black Power Movement in the United States and the work of Dr. Martin Luther King greatly influenced the mass struggle against an unpopular regime.

Yet another response to conditions of the 1960s was the dramatic growth of the Rastafarian Movement, whose philosophy drew heavily on the teachings of Marcus Garvey. Beckford and Witter (1980, p. 77) argue that it was Garvey who most graphically posed the problem of national oppression of the African peoples. Most of Garvey's philosophy was embraced by the Rastafarians on the island.

The Rastafarian Movement, in particular rejects "official" culture and ways in which European legacies dictated beliefs, tastes, and cultural patterns. For those who were socially alienated, economically deprived, and politically marginalized, the Rastafarians' counter-culture became an attractive vehicle of protest. It is fair to conclude that all aspects of the Rastafarian counter-culture went beyond its size to influence many middle-class youth. Further,

It was obviously an attractive ideology to the unemployed so far as it denounced the society that marginalised them. Many of them (middle-class youth) were sensitive to their ambiguous place in a sharply divided society, not rich, not poor,...neither black, nor white. The reaffirmation of their Africaness and the interpretation of their Christianity as a philosophy of social protest made Rastafari a ready ideology for coping with their socio-cultural alienation (Beckford and Witter 1980: 77).

Repression, poverty, and political alienation of the black majority all contributed to social unrest and rioting in 1968, which created a solidarity of position against the Jamaica Labour Party, headed by Prime Minister Hugh Shearer. The Prime Minister was often referred to as "Pharaoh," which in biblical terms, as well as Jamaican parlance, meant, "oppressor."

Then, social ferment and popular hostilities to the government found avenues of expression through popular culture, particularly music.

Jamaican singer Jimmy Cliff had earlier recorded "Suffering in the Land." Bob Andy spoke of repatriation with "Got To Go Back Home," while the Melodians, a popular group, sang of the disenchanted by the "Rivers of Babylon." Very popular too, was "Carry Go Bring Come," which asks, "How long shall the wicked reign over my people?" P.J. Patterson remembers:

Whenever that song was played at a party, it was enjoyed with particular gusto, not merely because it happened to be a very attractive song, but it also gave people an outlet for expressing themselves with loud refrain to "How long shall the wicked reign over my people?" (Interview, Patterson, 1987).

Fueled mainly by the rapid deterioration of social services, with a rise in social discontent, many other artists produced popular songs which well summed up the times. The most popular in late 1968 was "Everything Crash," which included these lines:

> Look deh now, everything crash!
> Firemen strike! Watermen strike!
> Telephone Company too!
> Down to the policemen too!
> What gone bad a mornin'
> Can't get good a evenin', oh
> Everyday carry bucket to the well
> One day the bucket bottom must drop out
> Everything crash, oh yeh,
> Me say look deh now.

The stage was now set for a new surge of hope among lower and middle income groups, ushering in a period of stronger association/involvement of local music in politics. The period of the late 1960s can be described as one of social protest, when social issues, particularly race, became the central focus of economic inequities and social disenchantment.

At the time of social ferment in the late 1960s, the People's National Party (PNP) changed its leader. Late National Hero Norman Washington Manley resigned, and his son, Michael, the trade unionist, was elected as the leader of the party in September 1969.

It was obvious that unless the PNP could mobilize all the disparate elements seeking change, including radical and progressive sentiments, the party would not have been able to unseat a government, unpopular at worst, but at best, tied to the country's largest trade union—the Bustamante Industrial Trades Union (BITU). As one source wrote:

Manley was able, therefore, to carefully construct a broad alliance of the nationalist and progressive elements within the local bourgeoisie, progressive elements of the middle class whose liberal political sentiments had been outraged by JLP repression, workers, peasants, unemployeds and other disaffected strata, such as Rastafari (Beckford and Witter 1980: 78).

All these disparate class interests came together under a multi-class alliance although Patterson could not recall any overt class or racial conflict in such an accommodation. He referred particularly to messages contained in local songs which would be unsettling for some elements of the local bourgeoisie.

I can't recall any performance which would have necessarily made any of the people associated with the party uncomfortable. That is to say there were no expressions of a racial kind. It doesn't mean, however, that people identified with a particular class position, they would not have received a clear warning that a change in the system was an absolute necessity (Interview, Patterson, 1987).

O.K. Melhado, a local business executive very much involved in the PNP's campaign until 1977, did not sense any discomfiture since people from all classes felt uneasy about the conditions then and thought a change was desirable. He said: "Even if you were from the upper class you were uncomfortable about the dichotomies and the situation that existed. So, I think there was a common chord which most people were comfortable with" (Interview, Melhado, 1987).

Clancy Eccles, artist and energetic organizer of the artists who supported the PNP's campaign, sensed that he was also part of an all-embracing coalition, stating, "I was aware of that. The big guys was a talk to me, the little guys was a talk to me, the Church of God, the Anglican" (Interview, Eccles, 1987).

So with rising social tension, a confluence of interests among all disaffected classes, and the election of the charismatic Michael Manley as leader of the PNP marked the beginning of the demise of the governing JLP. Music was to play an important role as themes contained in popular songs used on bandwagons became buzzwords throughout the campaign.

The Musical Bandwagon

There is consensus among activists that the idea for a bandwagon of popular artists to support the political hustlings of the PNP sprung from two events. First, Manley returned from an African tour with a walking stick given to him by the late Emperor Haile Selassie. The stick was dubbed the "Rod of Correction." Secondly, Clancy Eccles' spontaneous performance of a song written about "The Rod" was performed toward the end of Manley's constituency conference at the Ward Theatre in August 1971—spontaneous because Eccles denies any knowledge of Manley's rod prior to his arrival at the theater. Patterson remembers that,

Those of use who were privileged to both hear the song for the first time and to see the popular reaction to it, recognized that music was a powerful instrument that had to be used in the political process (Interview, Patterson, 1987).

Melhado was equally clear about how the music ought to be used:

If we could tie the music to meetings, this would be a tremendous attraction and it was what people were thinking. It was coming out of the artists' movement and that was the important thing. This fitted quite nicely with the party's agenda (Interview, Melhado, 1987).

Clancy Eccles, who was mainly responsible for mobilizing support among local talent, worked with Buddy Pouyatt and Paul Fitz-Ritson, both responsible for organization and finance of the bandwagon shows.

No formal contracts were signed as those attracted to Rastafarian ideas deeply distrusted "babylon papers." A promise to perform was sufficient. Performers on the musical bandwagon were among the leading songwriters and singers, later to become the outstanding exponents of reggae, locally and internationally. They included Bob Marley, Bunny Livingston, Peter Tosh, B.B. Seaton, Max Romeo, Clancy Eccles, Judy Mowatt, Ken Boothe, Scotty and the Chosen Few, Delroy Wilson, and Junior Byles.

It was generally expected that the main party machinery would create slogans and themes so the musical messages were consistent with official party sentiment. In fact, some of the key buzzwords used by PNP spokesmen came directly from artists who appeared at party-sponsored concerts. A typical example is Delroy Wilson's "Better Must Come" which became a big party slogan.

> I've been tying for a long long time,
> Still I can't make it
> Everything I try to do, seems to go wrong.
> It seems I have done something wrong,
> Why they trying to keep me down
> Who God bless no one curse
> Thank God I am not the worst
> Better must come, one day, better must come
> They can't conquer me, better must come.

Patterson, responding to whether the party influenced the songwriters by instructing what to write, said: "The song came first and we picked it from the song. We did not as members of the political directorate go to them with themes and lines. They came up with the song from which we drew inspiration" (Interview, Patterson, 1987).

Another song which enjoyed popularity on the campaign trail was Max Romeo's "Let the Power Fall on I," the lines of which stated:

> O let the power fall on I, Fari
> Let the power fall on I

Let the power from Zion fall on I
Let the power fall on I

O give I justice, peace and love, Fari
Give I justice, peace and love
Tell I how long will the wicked reign, Fari
Give I justice, peace and love

Romeo's wish for peace and justice was an apt political call in a violence-prone society deeply divided by class and race. However, other songs dealt with less divine intervention, pointing to personal or political destruction of a system not serving the best interests of a growing underclass. An example is:

Say me noh like dem kind a Babylon
Say me noh dig dem wicked men
For I'm a righteous Rastaman
And I'm a dread dread one I-man
I an' I go beat down Babylon
I an' I go whip dem wicked men.

O what a wicked situation
I an' I dying from starvation
This might cause a revolution
And a dangerous pollution
I an' go beat down Babylon
I an' go whip dem wicked men.

Waters (1985) was correct to claim that "Beat Down Babylon" by Junior Byles, addressed the lack of material wealth and warned of imminent revolution. This was another song banned but nevertheless played several times by DJs on the government-owned Jamaican Broadcasting Corporation (JBC).

On the eve of the elections, Peter Tosh, always seen as the most radical of the "Wailers," and subject to many police beatings, openly declared what results he was expecting:

Now that yu waited
Till you back is agains' the wall
One step to progress my brother I know
Jah will help you all.
Tell me how long
Must the good suffer for the bad
And everytime the good open his mouth
The bad say you musah (must be) mad
Dem ha fe get a beatin'
They have been reigning too long
It has been 400 years and

I just can't get on
Dem ha fe get a beatin'.

It is safe to say that the most popular songs of the period—on and off the charts—contained anti-government sentiments that helped seal the fate of the governing Jamaican Labour Party, founded by national hero and popular labour leader, Sir Alexander Bustamante.

The PNP won the 1972 elections by gaining 43 of 53 seats, with support from a broad cross-section of the 56.4 percent of the electorate.

Conclusion

The importance of popular culture in political discourse is further strengthened by its continued use in election campaigns. However, later attempts have been less organized and concentrated than in 1972. Eccles, obviously disappointed at what he considered to be insufficient benefits from state largesse, credited the use of popular music as the sole reason for the PNP's victory at the polls. He said, "Well without the music dem wouldn't win. We know that. Dem would remain opposition and get about twenty seats. The music is the most vital part of all campaign. That is why they always use the artists' tunes to do something" (Interview, Eccles, 1987).

Melhado, on the other hand, felt the music was a great mobilizing instrument, and Patterson placed it as an intrinsic part of the campaign, saying it "created a mood. It created a momentum."

However popular music is assessed, there is no denying its propensity for expressing popular feeling and class sentiments or having the ability to confer legitimacy on individuals or organizations seeking social and political change.

In the Jamaican case, the use of pop artists, along with a cultural expression so close to the majority population, assisted in mobilizing support for the victorious PNP. It is also important to note though that an aspect of popular culture was used to reflect deeply held sentiments of the predominantly black population, most of whom are responsible for deciding the outcome of elections in Jamaica.

Chapter Eight
Specialized Content and Narrative Structure in the Radio Dramas of Elaine Perkins of Jamaica

Maisha L. Hazzard
and
Vibert C. Cambridge

Introduction

Prior to independence, many Anglophone Caribbean radio systems featured soap operas as a major element of their programming. The majority of those very popular productions came from the Grace Gibson Studios in Australia or were local programming placements of British Broadcasting Corporation (BBC) productions.

The audience's preference for radio drama formats, particularly the serial soap opera format, can be traced to the early years of radio in the region. In Jamaica, for example, radio arrived November 17, 1939, "when John F. Grinan, an American, established an amateur radio station with the call letters NJ2 PZ" in St. Andrew Parish (Lynn 1981). When this radio station was bought by the colonial government in 1940 and renamed ZQ1, it "had an expanded programme schedule which included BBC World News, local news clipped from the pages of *The Gleaner* newspaper of Jamaica, and drama and comedy serials from Britain" (Lynn 1981:15).

In 1946, commercial radio began in Jamaica as a product of the privately-owned British Rediffusion International Limited with counterparts in St. Lucia, Barbados, Trinidad and Tobago, and British Guiana. Rafiq Khan, former general manager of Rediffusion's Radio Demerara in the now-independent Guyana, noted the development of the serial audiences in the Regional Rediffusion model:

We began with Grace Gibson's "Second Spring" in about 1949, and continued with "Portia Faces Life," "Aunt Mary," and "Dr. Paul." By the time these series ended in the early 1960s, we had developed a tremendous appetite in the region for this type of programme. (Interview, Khan, 1988)

In 1955, the colonial administration withdrew, and a new one advanced in Jamaica. The new government "did not regard a private commercial radio station, as had developed under the privately operated Rediffusion Limited, as sufficient to fulfill national needs and expectations" (Lynn 1981: 17). As leaders looked towards independence and the quest for consolidation of a national identity, criticism was directed at those vehicles that were developing and sustaining alien values and lifestyles. Nonetheless, Radio Jamaica Rediffusion (RJR) remained the uncontested commercial radio enterprise until 1959, with a continuation of programming featuring European classical music programs hosted by Jamaicans who were "caricatures of BBC stereotypes."

The objectives of Radio Jamaica Rediffusion Ltd. (RJR) were not directed to address national needs but to turn a profit. There was little evidence of social responsibility in programming prior to 1954 when time was allocated for political broadcasts in the transitional period in government.

At the point of transfer of administrative power in 1955, a very young Elaine Perkins began her career in Jamaican media as a reporter for a weekly newspaper, *Public Opinion*, and a weekly news magazine, *Spotlight*. By 1958, Perkins was writing short stories and features and conducting interviews as a freelancer for *The Daily Gleaner* and BBC. When events of 1959 opened radio to distinctively Jamaican voices, Perkins was poised and ready to heed the call (Interview, Perkins 1986).

In June 1959, RJR's monopoly of Jamaican airwaves ended when a public station, Jamaica Broadcasting Corporation, was established "to provide an outlet for Jamaican culture, a forum for discussion of public affairs, and an additional means of education" (Lynn 1981).

Within the context of this new development in Jamaican radio, Perkins joined JBC as a scriptwriter, writing features on literacy, prison reform, agricultural development, and matters concerning government policy. From time to time, she employed dramatic story telling:

I used to do little half hour and fifteen minute playlets which didn't push the message down anybody's throat. They were never to know that this was—unless I couldn't help it—what it was about. It would be a normal little story. I didn't necessarily even have to mention the name of the thing that I was dealing with, but by constructing the story and selecting the characters and what happens to them, the story became the message. (Perkins 1987a)

Most of those early playlets lacked continuity because they were usually self-contained vignettes interspersed in the JBC format that primarily utilized the magazine shows, documentaries, talk shows, commentaries, and speeches by government officials (Interview, Perkins, 1986). But, one dramatic program, developed as part of the government's mosquito eradication campaign, established Perkins' reputation as a serial writer who could achieve results. Perkins stated that she called the short serial, "Raymond, the Sprayman," which she created to specifically address "the problem with the Aedes Egypt mosquito which caused a lot of health problems like dengue fever and various types of influenza" (Interview, Perkins, 1986). Problems were due to incubation of mosquitos in stagnant water repositories in houses and yards. Perkins' task was to convince people to admit health inspectors to their homes "with their little spray guns." Jamaican people had resisted inspection and extermination procedures because "the people believed that the spray would poison them, harm their children, destroy their food and crops, and destroy their animals" (Perkins 1987a). "Raymond, the Sprayman's" job was "to go into these areas every week for fifteen minutes" during a six-week period. In the show, he would meet a different set of characters each week who represented the opposition that real health officers and spraymen were confronting.

Perkins used humor to capture the attention and soften the resistance. "Raymond, the Sprayman" was described by Perkins as a "sort of Charlie Chaplin character. He was always mixing up things using the wrong spray, falling down, and mixing up people's things." But, eventually "he would get his way after going through all sorts of pitfalls and escapades with the various characters who would resist him." That program achieved results, as many people who previously had not let the spraymen in, were receptive to them. After that, Perkins employed dramatic technique, often in projects on prisons and literacy, more in single episodes than multi part series.

In 1962, a new government under independent rule took office in Jamaica. Head of state, Norman Manley, appointed a minister of development who

devised something called Farmers' Productive, the government five-year plan. It was mainly a rural plan to get the whole farming community to stop being superstitious about things like fertilizer and [to stop resisting] agricultural extension officers who would teach them things about terracing, new crops, new methods of agriculture, and adult literacy. (Perkins 1987a)

In 1963, the Jamaican government established the Jamaica Information Service (JIS), following the introduction of the 1963 Broadcasting Regulations. The Jamaica Information Service (JIS) was designed to "keep Jamaica informed about the plans, policies and day-to-day activities of the government" (Forrestor 1977). It was to facilitate development operations being carried out by the ministry of development and other state agencies.

Elaine Perkins' success as a scriptwriter and producer, whose work reflected the voices and concerns of the target audiences, led to her appointment as acting broadcasting officer at JIS. Perkins supervised staff producers involved in the production of "Science Corner," "Art Corner," "Things Jamaican," "Portfolio," "Country Life," and "Between the Lines." She developed documentaries, talk shows, art programs, historical series on Jamaica, and dramatic programs.

JIS developed campaigns that included radio, magazines, group discussions, flip charts, and other media. Perkins provided a radio integration of specialized content presented through the other forms. JIS was to inform people about new health centers being placed within eight miles of every village, agricultural projects, literacy programs, and numerous other services (Perkins 1987a).

Initially, the rural development projects were presented in the radio magazine show, "Country Life." Elaine Perkins was overwhelmed by the task of presenting information on literacy, fertilizers, artificial insemination, and numerous other projects because it seemed to require that she "do one little half hour program on literacy, one on fertilizer, one on this, one on that." She decided instead to "create a village. I'm just going to create some people and put them in a place and everything there will happen to them. They'll need fertilizer, they'll die, need to go to school, be sick, need roads, and it will just come naturally" (Perkins 1987a).

The interrelatedness of issues affecting the adoption of innovations and receptivity to information was clear to Perkins. Problems with lapsed literacy[1] limited access to information that might have conditioned openness to new ideas and procedures. Folk beliefs and superstitions seemed to prevail in environments with limited information access. Top-down presentation of development programs sometimes incited rejection as deficiencies in information acquiring skills were underscored by confrontations with formally educated officials. Self concept, pride, self determination, self respect, and self sufficiency were perceived by Perkins as some of the underlying motivations for program rejection or acceptance.

The Evolution of a Formula

Elaine Perkins created "Hopeful Village," a serial that ran for ten years on JBC. She wrote and produced the show for the first four years before moving on to the commercial serial, "Stella" (1967-1968), and Jamaica's longest running, most successful soap opera to date, "Dulcimina—Her Life in Town" (1967– 1980).

Both "Stella" and "Dulcimina—Her Life in Town" represented a departure from development-oriented work that Perkins had done for JIS which later became the Agency for Public Information, API. "Stella," based on a murder mystery depicted the romantic problems of an educated, middle-class woman in Jamaica. The series competed with Perkins' own "Dulcimina," a daily soap, that chronicled the struggles, triumphs, and defeats of rural Jamaicans who were moving to the urban centers in vast numbers. Although "Dulcimina" was independent of JIS demands for development themes, the serial addressed the challenges of urban survival amidst unemployment, housing crises, cultural adaptations in the face of differing lifestyles and values, difficulties with food provisions, and other conditions stemming from the urban-rural dialectic. "Dulcimina" was broadcast for four years on JBC before political pressures and unsatisfactory financial arrangements led to its transfer to RJR in 1971. Nevertheless, "Dulcimina" remains the uncontested, premier success of indigenous serial drama in Jamaican radio history.

Through the creation of these early works, Perkins tested formulas for the development of believable characters that became the vehicles for development themes in her more recent serials, "Life at the Mimosa Hotel" (1984) and "Naseberry Street" (1985 to present). "Life at the Mimosa Hotel" was created for the Joan Williams and Associates Advertising Agency and the Jamaica Tourist Board for broadcast on JBC. Set in a small hotel on the North Coast, that weekly series was designed "to modify attitudes and behaviors of street vendors towards tourists in Jamaica." "Life at the Mimosa Hotel" depicted the struggles of hotel owners, legitimate vendors, and tourists against harassment from "higglers" (previously non-legitimized street vendors). The program was cancelled while peaking in audience polls because of political disfavor incurred by Perkins' husband, provocative journalist, Wilmot Perkins. His frequent controversial political analyses allegedly also led to the cancellation in 1980 of "Dulcimina—Her Life in Town."

Both "Life at the Mimosa Hotel" and "Naseberry Street" enjoyed success. "Naseberry Street," produced for the Jamaica Family Planning Association, has had great impact on family planning campaigns as evidenced in data from 1986 audience surveys and family planning program monitoring. "Naseberry Street," broadcast on RJR[2], is set on Naseberry Street in a low income urban community in Jamaica. The serial features the ongoing story of the women in the yards, the men who father their children, and the prices they pay for "careless love" (Interview, Perkins, 1986).

Steps in Creation of the Perkins Serial

When Elaine Perkins presented a seminar on serial development for the Johns Hopkins Population Communication Programme in Trinidad in August 1987, she outlined the guidelines of a commercially-viable script, its content and format. She explained: the need to convince people that they are in charge of their own lives, and to see themselves in the situations and characters in the drama; the considerations for the audience, age group, income levels, urban or rural location, characteristics, family structures, literacy, religion/superstition; the creation of themes and characters around conflict and drama; the development of environments for characters to live in with pertinent details; the creation of prototypes for key characters, and the details of differentiation for target audience and mass audience (Johns Hopkins University 1987).

When discussing the planning of development serials, Perkins outlined additional instructions. She said the soap opera must have: an educational lever (specific content/information and purpose), realistic characters, exciting plot developed for the ear, a mechanism to enable a recap of each episode, sharp, vivid, descriptive dialogue (think of audience as being blind), and commercial appeal (elements that create interest in audience so that they listen voluntarily). Others that she added were: clearly-defined characters whose role is determined by the message to be imparted by that character and whose speech and behaviors are consistent within a logical line of development and growth, story outlines that develop motivated actions, behaviors, plot complications, relationships before scripting, limited number of plots, subplots and ideas plus controlled pacing, quality production values that communicate realism to the audience, carefully utilized sound effects that establish time and place without distracting from the plot development, economy in the use of dialogue to prevent excessive verbiage that could detract from the storyline, relationships, and characterization, and blended elements (specialized content, production values and elements, storylines and characterization).[3]

Target Audience Analysis

In lectures at Ohio University, Perkins outlined her process, which begins with close scrutiny of her target audience. While describing the development of "Hopeful Village," Perkins discussed her deliberations:

I decided what income level I was going to win over, in what part of the country they were. I started to think about how they thought, how they spoke because we have a vernacular; we have a dialect and although everybody on the whole island speaks dialect, there are certain little features—little things that are peculiar and certain beliefs, too, that are peculiar to certain rural areas. [There are] little superstitions. You'll find one place will call a ghost a dobie and another will call it a duppy. Keeping those things in mind, I try to get into their heads. (Perkins 1987a)

Perkins employed similar strategies in preparation for "Stella," "Dulcimina—Her Life in Town," "Life at the Mimosa Hotel," and "Naseberry Street." In 1985, Perkins developed the "Naseberry Street" pilot after identifying her target audience.

I sat down and thought about the demographics. I knew there was no need to tell the middle class, upwardly mobile about family planning. The type I am really appealing to is the young, unexposed, [informally educated] with superstitious beliefs [about family planning]—those with mental barriers. (Perkins 1987a)

She elected underclass women of child bearing years (12 to 45 years old) and explored their attitudes, beliefs, and practices related to sexuality, intimacy, family planning, child bearing and rearing, male-female relationships, goals and aspirations, life styles, and patterns of interaction, style and language of communication, patterns of education, and of relationships with health service personnel and traditional health attendants.

Perkins intuitively acknowledged several issues at the root of many relationships leading to pregnancy out of wedlock, or frequent pregnancy in marriage: low self-esteem, beliefs of men that various birth control methods will render them impotent, fear of state-organized genocide of Black people, need for money or shelter (returned for sexual "favors"), craving for affection and love, lack of substantive information about methods of availability, conflicts about preparing to indulge in unsanctioned intimacy,[4] influence of superstitious, traditional health attendants,[5] and fear of deleterious results from the introduction of artificial (unnatural) measures of birth control.

Armed with a knowledge of attitudes and beliefs contributing to resistance to family planning measures, Perkins set out to create a world of people representing some of the traditional beliefs as well as the new beliefs and understanding.

Creating the World of the Serial

To create a world that would be consistent and well defined, the writer/producer/director acquired a plan of operation for "Hopeful Village" which she has used for subsequent serials. In an attempt to create a world upon which the audience might eavesdrop via radio, Perkins established the environment for her archetypal characters:

First of all, I actually drew a map. This is Hopeful Village. This is where the shop is. This is how far it is from the shop to the bus stop. This is where the bus driver lives, the health center, the community center, so that I knew where everybody was and how they related to each other. (Perkins 1987a)

The hub of Perkins' "Hopeful Village" was the local shop where people could leave and receive messages, post mail, buy weekly supplies, stop for conversation on the way home for the bus stop, and give or get the latest news. The shop, the church, and various other locations were logical and familiar settings for the types of action and dialogue spawned in the serial.

The hotel "hub" in "Life at the Mimosa Hotel" typified the settings where hotel owners, service personnel, tourists, business people, and "higglers" meet. It was the ideal locale for the types of conflicts and resolutions that the Jamaica Tourist Board needed to have presented in sensitive ways, hoping that Jamaicans would view the tourist industry as a key component in their personal and national economic development.

When "Naseberry Street" was on the drawing board, Perkins said she "selected a street, 'Naseberry Street.' This street had a number of yards populated by a lot of women in child bearing years (12-45). I created a street in which there is a clinic, a family planning clinic, because I need a center, but I'm not pushing" (Perkins 1987a).

On the street, with yards in close proximity, live a nurse from the clinic, who has her own problems, and a traditional health attendant, with her teenage granddaughter. Those two characters bring many young women into the scene as they administer health care. The predominance of young women on the block is a lure for young and old men with various motives and different senses of responsibility and respect for women.

Naseberry Street is a typical street in town with transient people residing amidst the core of long-term, deeply-entrenched neighbors. Action takes place on the street, in front of houses and yards, in the houses, and in the clinic.

Content: Integrating Themes, Storylines,
Information in Character Driven Drama

Perkins noted that the concept of the development drama was to make it not sound like propaganda:

There was never any suggestion—there could never be any suggestion—that we were pushing things down people's throats. It had to come about as part of the lives of the characters, the things that motivated them as they saw themselves, the way they lived their lives. This is what I have to do: I have the information—all of the information—all of the research. I have to compress [the research] and break it down in ways that I know would be easily assimilated. (Perkins 1987a)

Perkins created characters whose lives automatically allowed for the unfolding of themes germane to the campaign. In "Hopeful Village," she created a farmer named Little John who "was about fifty, and was very set in his traditional farming ways." Little John epitomized the rural person who was the "obstructionist" in government development programs. She added:

He didn't believe in fertilizer. He said that made the yams too big and the yams would poison people. He wouldn't allow his crops to be artificially inseminated. He was also what we call a lapsed literate in that he had been to school but had left school at about thirteen and he couldn't read. But, nobody knew he couldn't read because he was so fabulous; he was numerate and could do all his accounts. [So he managed] to keep his illiteracy a secret. Nobody knew except perhaps his immediate family. (Perkins 1987a)

The storylines that involved Little John allowed for the development of themes related to his lack of understanding of innovations because of his lapsed literacy and limited exposure. Within the context of the drama, Little John had to confront issues involving his self concept, his respected community position, his secret of illiteracy, his vulnerability resulting from his illiteracy, and his entrenchment in tradition because of a fear of incompetence in a realm requiring formal education skills like reading. Perkins said:

There was this one day he wanted to find something to get rid of ticks on his animals and he went to the store and bought it. He came home and used it on the animals and the ticks didn't go away. He said it was no good. The story builds up over a period of weeks. Another friend, equally illiterate, told him "I know that thing. That thing is a thing that has to be drunk. You've bought the wrong thing." [Little John] drank some of [the potion] because he couldn't read the label, and he became ill. I was trying to prove, in that instance, the value of adult literacy. I was trying to get them to go back to school. (Perkins 1987a)

Little John became a role model for new possibilities and growth. According to Perkins, as long as the conflicts and resolutions evolve out of the characters realistically, audience members with similar dilemmas can grow with them. The entire dynamic process seems to have worked most effectively when it has taken place over an extended period of character and plot development.

In the case of "Naseberry Street," the premise was clear to Perkins: "Family planning is good for you. It is in your best interest." With that in mind, a set of characters was developed to provide spokespersons for particular world views and carry the messages of the campaign through a growth process that illuminated the problems caused by failure to plan families. ·

The character, Nana, was created to embody community resistance to family planning based on traditional beliefs and superstitions. Perkins said she created her as a neighbor to the family planning nurse from the clinic. An old midwife who is very superstitious, she believes that "women are born to have a certain amount of children—failure to do so will result in sickness" (Perkins 1987a). When she ties the baby's umbilical cord, she says things like "I see ten knots; this means you will have ten more children."

Nana becomes the arch enemy of the family planning campaign. She symbolizes the superstitions that impede progress, yet, Perkins' approach is not to "stomp her down," so to speak, but to challenge her erroneous ideas gradually. Evidence is presented to refute her perspective and offer other possibilities for women in their child-bearing years. Nana spouts the negative superstitions: "contraceptives make the man sick;" "God has the plan for your life and will punish you if you leave His way;" "God will provide for whatever number you have;" "good girls don't need to have anything because they won't do anything wrong; if you prepare, it's because you intend to sin." Nana is the first and most formidable opponent of the village nurse, but Nana is not all wrong nor all bad. She represents the folk wisdom of the people, has legitimate knowledge of traditional cures and practices that work, and is perceptive in many situations and accurate in some of her assessments.

The nurse represents modern wisdom, born of scientific discoveries and demonstrated in health-saving innovations. While she brings knowledge and expertise to Naseberry Street, she is not without faults or limitations; for example, her social analysis is often biased. She has raised a son who impregnates a young woman and is convicted for conspiring to defraud poor people in a housing scam. The nurse's reality reflects the normal vicissitudes of life experienced by her neighbors, yet, she provides a direct connection to the family planning clinic and can occasionally be heard offering perspectives that are essential for young women contemplating their responsibilities for personal family planning.

In episode 306, to illustrate Perkins' manipulation of character and storylines, the nurse shows her vulnerability, that she is not above the rest of the residents on Naseberry Street.

Nurse: People ask how I feel, if I'm all right, that I must take it easy. They tell me not to worry because it will send up my pressure, or make me mad. I've never complained before. I've never told anybody what it feels like to have a child who is always giving me trouble, but I'm feeling it. And I know it is not me alone.

This characteristic problem with her son creates a sympathetic relationship with the audience, who might assume professional women like Nurse Hugget cannot understand their plight because of their own idyllic life. But Nurse Hugget suffers her own problems with a son who strings several women along, fathers children by several of them, and exploits the hopes of the poor with confidence games.

Mr. Plummer of "Naseberry Street" is an older man who is a respected business man and church elder. He has seduced his grandniece, Donna, who is pregnant by him. She threatens to blackmail him as indicated in Plummer's narration at the beginning of episode #170:

Plummer: I had to go and see Donna tonight, cool her down with some money just to keep her quiet until I get through with my little business with Judge Layton. Imagine, she claims she pregnant for me and she want to have the baby. But what she have over me is a threat...yes...and it serve me right, cause I thought she was a decent little girl and I start fool around her, nevva know she was such a gold digger. She going to tell her mother how I seduce her. And I mean to say, that not gwine sound good, not to my lodge brother, not to Judge Layton. It going to mash up my business too, cause Donna's mother is really my sister's eldest daughter's daughter. Therefore, Donna is to call me grand uncle, so to speak.

Audience members listen in on various sides of Plummer's thoughts and actions. They hear him here without remorse for his incestuous seduction but with concern for his position in the community. They hear his involvements with the daughters of church members. As a result, they perceive him as an exploiter of young women who allow themselves to be used by him for money or father love in an environment where many men have departed for work in the U.S. or elsewhere. Plummer is brought down by Perkins eventually, as evidence against his honor mounts week by week. The audience hears him in the midst of his lascivious acts of seduction and grow to abhor his behavior and admonish the women who are taken in by his money and his sweet talk. By episode #309, Plummer's culpability is at least partially known. The audience is aware, but the characters have yet to uncover the full measure of his lecherous nature.

In episode #309, Perkins also shows the Nurse working with a young girl who is the perfect prey for Plummer. The eldest of several children, the girl has been reported to the nurse for truancy by her teacher who suspects that she is meeting secretly with her boyfriend. Nurse, who sees all of the traits of a prospective victim, helps the girl clarify her values and reaffirm her commitment to her goals and aspirations.

Nurse: You helping out [her mother with her siblings]? Now you see the responsibility that you are in? Your mother is working out, your father is abroad, working hard to try and send for you. You are in school, you have ambition, right?
Girl: Yes Nurse.
Nurse: You want to have a profession. You want to have a career. Have you thought about that?
Girl: Yes.
Nurse: What?
Girl: I want to study computer.
Nurse: Now that's very good. Now if you have a goal like that, and you see how conditions are with your mother. You see how she have it hard, oh, but you see the responsibility that is placed upon you. You have responsibility to yourself first—to be the best person that you can be. Try and stay in school.

Nurse continues to question the girl about her relationship with her boyfriend and to point out dangers and temptations: "You find yourself with a stomach. What you think would happen to you. Your father would be disgusted. Standford is a school boy, right. Him can't help you, so postpone things, right." She tells the girl that the teacher thinks she has a great future and the girl "begins to laugh in a proud sort of way."

In that scene, which is a natural one for the Naseberry clinic, Perkins articulates dreams and possibilities for young women who may not have looked beyond the day at hand to see how they can direct their futures, rather than simply allowing them to unfold without direction. This scene is in the same episode as a scene in which Nurse refers to Mr. Plummer's liaisons with Princess and the daughter of one of the church sisters.

Summary, Inferences, and Recommendations

Elaine Perkins' work provides a functional model for development communication projects. Her serial, "Naseberry Street," has an audience of 1 million out of a population of 2.5 million, according to recent audience surveys. According to Jamaica Family Affiliation data, as reported by Perkins, birth rates are going down and more women have enrolled in adult education programs, or participate in special programs for women, such as The Sistrens.[6]

Without mentioning the development issue, it is possible to confront the underlying issues that affect the acceptance or rejection of ideas, information, and innovations. Elaine Perkins has stated that she is not "selling family planning"; she is selling understanding, possibilities, dreams of self respect, and self determination, and family planning is simply offered as a means to those ends.

In all the sample episodes read and listened to, Perkins has woven a complex tapestry of story ideas that emerge naturally from her characters. Each character seems to serve a function. For example:

Character   Role (to depict)

Nana: Traditional beliefs

Nurse: Official family planning ideas as well as common middle class, middle age dilemmas for women

Plummer: Lecherous old men who take advantage of the vulnerability, youth, and poverty of young women

Scattershot: Sweet talking, charming seducer of women who thrives on having many women fighting over him and giving birth to his children, for whom he accepts little responsibility

Laverne: Young women with ambition, vision, and insight

Girl: Young, inexperienced girls who have not made their choices yet—who have dreams and potential that can only be realized if they exercise power over their own lives and make conscious decisions to plan their lives

Wallace: Religious mothers who think that praying and going to church and simply talking to their daughters about God's will and what good girls do will prevent the avoidable.

Each character is a catalyst for the development of various themes: need for self respect, self determination, self development, and self control; need for openness to new ideas, education, warmth and affection, information, comprehension, freedom from erroneous ideas; right to respect from others, fair treatment, opportunities, protection, guidance; freedom to choose, to act. Each story line establishes the interrelatedness of education and understanding of innovations, exposure and openness to new ideas, skill development and self respect, need for affection and careless sexual relationships, fear and adherence to traditional methods, poor self esteem and low or no goal direction, hopelessness and seeming helplessness, a sense of powerlessness and victimization.

Characters who are formidable opponents of the development plan must be created so that growth in acceptance, or at least growth in perspective, can be demonstrated over time through character and plot development. Conflicts can reveal motives and objectives. Triumph over obstacles can demonstrate possibilities for problem solving for audience if characters are realistic, identifiable, and consistent in their growth patterns.

These characters need to be studied over a three to five year period to determine the growth patterns—the dynamics in character development. Work on "Naseberry Street" has just begun, but it is clear that Perkins has tapped a source of inspiration which she can offer to development communication specialists and audiences throughout the world.

The characters created by Perkins are dynamic and multi-dimensional. She exploits the magic of the eavesdropping reality of media serials by deliberately allowing listeners to be privy to intimate details of each character's life in a variety of settings. This is perhaps the most crucial aspect of the serial as a development tool because listeners have characters under surveillance in situations that provide information about their true natures. Plummer can be seen in his role as the outstanding citizen, the church elder, the prosperous and responsible business man, and the seducer and exploiter of young women. This is a vital way to bring to fore the masks that some people wear, the hidden dimensions of individuals that would be known to few, and the covert motives of characters who share their intimate thoughts and actions.

More is learned about the characters of the serial drama than real people usually learn about people they know. Listeners can hear in "Naseberry Street," the infamous character, Scattershot, as he lures women into his lair. Consumers witness him laughing about his conquests with his male friends and bragging about his children whose names he cannot always remember. The character is exposed in ways real people seldom are. This is the fundamental power of the serial needing systematic study; it is perhaps at the crux of listener commitment and loyalty.

Listeners do know the characters in the serials better than they know real people. They are poised in the seat of omniscience at the periphery of an electronic world, and there is the powerful insight that comes with privileged knowledge. It is this that Elaine Perkins casts as her net over the masses of Jamaicans in her audience.

Chapter Nine
Radyo Tanbou:
The Function of the Popular Media in Guadeloupe

Alvina Ruprecht

Radio broadcasting, as opposed to television or print media, reaches the broadest spectrum of the Guadeloupean population and thus provides a great variety of channels for the cultural reality of the island. In these circumstances, it would seem perfectly acceptable to refer to radio as an instance of popular culture. However, the notion of "popular" seems extremely restrictive in this particular context where cultural practices are determined as much by questions of economic stratification as by a vision of the world resulting from the complex set of relationships between the metropolitan "culture française" and an ethnically specific configuration of cultural expressions. In order to discuss radio broadcasting as one of these cultural instances, we must first come to terms with the evasive notion of popular culture.

In the broadest anthropological sense, culture refers to all symbolic activity of human beings: artistic expression, ideas, concepts, symbolic behaviour, etc. The more restrictive notion of popular culture, often related to mass culture of which radio is a component, appears contradictory. It amalgamates many phenomena, including traditional artistic expression, modern folk art, as well as qualities supposedly inherent in mass media products of cinema, television, radio programs, and any artistic endeavor considered as escapist entertainment. Popular culture also refers to group phenomena which cut across class boundaries, whereas in other contexts, popular culture is defined in a binary formation which presupposes class distinctions: popular culture as opposed to elitist or official culture, distinctions seen by some as reflecting an "outmoded romantic notion of the cult of the people" (Barbu 1976: 65). These questions have been discussed at great length by Leo Lowenthal (1961), Stuart Hall (1965), Zev Barbu (1976), and S.L. Kaplan (1984).

Background on Guadeloupe

120

As our attention will be focussing on one particular example of radio broadcasting (Radyo Tanbou), in a particular geographical location, it would seem useful to reconsider these general definitions in the light of the specific conditions of existence which produced this radio station.

Guadeloupe is a French and Creole-speaking island structurally integrated into the social, legal, and political institutions of France. This long-distance departmental relationship is defined as "colonial" by many Guadeloupean intellectuals, artists, and critics. They feel the French Metropolitan government imposes conditions which do not take into account their cultural specificity, determined by the interaction of various ethnic groups of which Europeans are not a majority. The consequences of this uneasy relationship between Metropolitan France and the inhabitants of the island, is a sense of cultural identity which often expresses itself locally in polemical terms.

For example, sociolinguist Dany Bebel-Gisler, continues in the line of thought of Balibar and Laporte (1974) who show that historically, the French have imposed linguistic uniformity as a mechanism of cultural eradication and political domination. Bebel-Gisler in her book *La Langue Créole, Force Jugulée* (1981) refers specifically to the exclusion of Creole from the school curriculum. This policy of French as the only legitimate national language is reflected in the official notion of "territorial continuity" and in statements such as the one made by the director of the state-financed radio station RFO (Radio France Outre mer) to the effect that Creole has no place on "national" radio because it is a "regional dialect and technically inadequate for weather and traffic reports" (Interview, Decrozes 1987).

In this context, cultural practices that can be manipulated by institutionalized forces, eventually turn into weapons wielded by all the protagonists. Writer Max Jeanne (1981, p. 134) states that "cultural practices will take over as political acts and help to forge a national conscience."

These kinds of confrontations are particularly significant within the media, which are seen as direct channels of Metropolitan culture on the island. In an attempt to provide a counter discourse, a French producer, Raoul Sangla, along with two journalists, Michel Reinette and Jean-Pierre Mabille, were asked by the "Conseil régional" to produce a series of experimental television programs on and about the island. It was called "Télévision-Caraïbes" and it was broadcast in January 1987 as a pirate television program. A series of 14 news magazines were filmed on location, each one in a different commune. Local people were interviewed about their particular problems: unemployment, irrigation, housing, racism and intermarriage, Metropolitan control of the media, participation of workers in management of local business, the function of the artist in society, good tourists and bad tourists, cooperative farming, excessive taxes, and immigrants. The point of these news magazines was to deal with subjects that are not normally presented on the authorized media, and above all, to hear what the local inhabitants had to say, without their opinions being filtered through a journalist or an official spokesman. This news format was, in fact, a challenge thrown out to the official media, because it offered an alternative form of information gathering which was not technically sophisticated but which allowed the authentic voice of the people to be heard. In other words, because of the tensions within this society, the making of these films as a simple expression of the cultural reality of Guadeloupean society could only be seen as a political act.

In the same order of ideas, writer Maryse Condé, speaking during hearings before the national radio and television licensing board (Commission nationale de la communication et des libertés) in November 1987, in support of a local television project, emphasized the need to "exercise and perfect one's own creativity without being reduced to the permanent consumption of the creativity of others." Here she was referring to the minimal amount of locally-produced television content (four hours monthly plus a 15-minute news bulletin five days a week) transmitted on the local television channel, RFO 1. Her point was to emphasize the need for a channel which would give priority to the dissemination of expressions of Guadeloupean culture, in a context where local culture is not considered valid by many of those who control the media outlets.

Underlying the way this whole question is approached by intellectuals of the French Caribbean and by the Metropolitan authorities, is Althusser's argument (1971) that components of what is called culture are best defined in ideological terms. Culture functions as an ideological construct within an apparatus, such as the media, through a subject which acts according to its own imaginary position in relation to the dominant system of beliefs of that society. In this context then, notions such as "popular culture" do not help us clarify things. On the contrary, they are much too restrictive. Definitions which take into account purely descriptive criteria, such as numbers of individuals or class distinctions, do not consider the power relationships, that over periods of time, are built into social and political structures by perceptions of differences not always related to economic inequalities. What seems more relevant here, is the way cultural technologies operate in relation to the whole ideological fabric of the state. Considered from this point of view then, radio broadcasting, as one of these technologies, plays an important role in defining what this power relationship might be and how it functions.

Guadeloupean Radio

There are 32 authorized private radio stations and several unauthorized stations operating in Guadeloupe. There is also one state-financed station (RFO), one semi-private station (RCI), and since January 1988, France-Inter (a state-owned channel) has been coming in directly from France via satellite on the AM band.

These broadcasting outlets represent a great variety of ideological positions. For example, Radio France Outre mer (RFO) posits that Guadeloupe is one regional sub-unit of Metropolitan culture defined in terms of the dominant national culture which is European French. This premise produces an information policy aimed at avoiding conflict and controversy because it does not recognize an opposing position. Radio Massabielle asserts that the Roman Catholic cultural tradition as a product of western values, provides the framework for all authentic culture. Symbolic activity from any other source is invalid. This point of view excludes a good portion of the cultural base of the Guadeloupean population which is not of Western origin.

Radio Gaiac frames all issues and cultural manifestations in terms of class struggle but focuses on this struggle in the local context. There are other smaller stations, such as Radio Bis, which function according to commercial free enterprise strategy. Radio, as a consumer product, must confirm the needs and desires of the affluent part of the population so that it can attract the right kinds of advertisers. There are, of course, many more.

Radyo Tanbou is of particular interest to us because of the results of a public opinion poll conducted by the Parisian agency SECODIP (Société d'études de la consommation, de la distribution et de la publicité) for Radio France Outre mer and published by *L'independans* (1986) the official organ of the U.P.L.G. (Union pour la libération de la Guadeloupe), an independence movement. According to this poll, 43 percent of the Guadeloupean listening audience was divided between RFO (the state-financed radio) and RCI (Radio Caraïbes international, financed by public and private Metropolitan interests); Radyo Tanbou, a locally-financed non-profit private radio, was third in the poll with 15. 8 percent of the listening audience. Given the enormous material advantages of the other two stations, working with teams of full time paid journalists[1], modern technology, and international news sources linked up to satellite, Radyo Tanbou's performance is phenomenal.

Founded in 1982, it is financed by "Le Mouvement patriotique," an umbrella group formed by local organizations that support the U.P.L.G. It is staffed by one news director, six journalists and about ten technicians. Only three of the employees are paid and the others have regular full time occupations, in most cases, as teachers. They spend about fourteen hours a week of their free time working at the station. Broadcasting is done with a minimal amount of equipment, set up in a small apartment on the fifteenth floor of a residential building in the center of Pointe-à-Pitre, the commercial capital of the island. Programming starts at 5:30 a.m. and continues till 10 p.m., with a break from 3 to 5 p.m., except on Wednesdays and Saturdays, when programming is not interrupted in the middle of the day (See Table 1).

Table 1

Weekly Program Schedule for Radyo Tanbou

Morning	Time	Content
	5h30	Music
	6h00	News headlines
	6h15	Public service announcements
	6h30	Local news
	7h00	News prolonged with interviews of special guests: politicians, specialists, etc. (20-30 minutes timing is flexible)
	8h00	Synthesis of local and Caribbean news
	8h30	Announcer changes. Programs vary according to the day of the week: discussion of public health questions or music (traditional, *Gwoka*, Latin American, African, American music with a progressive content, popular music of the French Caribbean, *Zouk*). Also included in this slot are programs for children and analysis of economic questions. Content varies also according to the availability of material.
	12h00	News headlines
	12h15	Local public service announcements
	12h30	Local news
	13h00	Public affairs magazine. Interview with a specialist in some field
Afternoon	Time	Content
	13h30	The technician takes over. He plays
	15h00	music, receives phone calls, tells stories, interviews people. He has complete freedom to do what he wants
	17h30	Information
	18h00	
Monday	18h30 etc.	Sports analysis, interviews, commentaries
Tuesday	18h30 etc.	Health and environment questions
Wednesday	15h00	Broadcast by the Teachers Union

	16h00	Spanish lesson
	17h00	Music
	20h00	Discussion of economic questions
		once a month is devoted to questions
		concerning the social security system
Thursday	18h30	Broadcast by the Association of Haïtian
		workers
Friday	18h30	Broadcast by a youth organization
Saturday	13h00	Resumé of weekly international events
		with emphasis on Third world
		countries
	16h00	Cultural program devoted to different
		aspects of Guadeloupean culture
18h00 etc	Music	

Sunday Programming

	5h30	Advice on the use of health products and
		natural foods
	7h30	"Kaw ka di de sa?" (What have you got to
		say about that?) Commentary and analysis
		of current controversial issues with
		open line phone-in
	9h30	Music
	10h00	"Grand Causer" Each week a different
	12h00	theme is the basis of a long discussion-
		literature, environment, health
		questions, and the Caribbean
	15h00	Sports and music
	18h00	Rebroadcast of Wednesday's Spanish lesson
	20h00	Rebroadcast of "What do you have to say
	22h00	about that?"

A close look at the broadcast schedule shows that there is very little content that could be called escapist or "easy listening," appealing to the spontaneous and the irrational, all the criteria corresponding to the generally—accepted definitions of mass media culture. There are no games or phone—in quizzes, regular fare on most of the other stations; there is no radio drama and on the weekdays, there is only an hour and a half of afternoon chit chat with a technician as host, who plays music and conducts interviews.

Music is used as "entertainment" and filler when other programming isn't available, but music has another role here as well, i.e. to validate local traditional culture. It emphasizes *Gwoka* (traditional drumming) and other forms of traditional music, but also plays modern music from different countries of Latin America, Africa, and areas of the U.S. to build cultural bridges that bypass the European-oriented relationship with the Métropole.

It is clear, however, that the bulk of the programming is made up of information: 90 minutes per day of news reports plus news magazines; interviews which often last half an hour or more; analysis, commentary, and in-depth discussions of current, often controversial questions. Far from providing escapist entertainment that makes no intellectual demands on the listener, most of their programming appears to be intellectually demanding and politically stimulating because it plunges the listener into the midst of the most heated debates of the day. A brief comparison with the local news content of the two other major radio stations provides some interesting results. RFO offers a maximum of 45 minutes per day of local news, but the content emphasizes events directly related to Metropolitan French institutions and official points of view. RCI, which is closely connected to Metropolitan political and financial interests, presents about 30 minutes per day of local news but it emphasizes human interest stories and Metropolitan-related events. Both stations avoid news of a conflictual nature, or else, if reported, it is often dealt with as a human interest story and not as politically relevant news, thus distancing the event from the listeners and transforming it into entertainment (see Appendix).

On the other hand, because Radyo Tanbou seeks out conflict not as emotionally-charged, escapist drama, but as a means of forcing listeners to take sides and, thus, become intellectually involved, it seems to represent everything that mass media culture is supposed to reject. In one sense then, it might be argued that Radyo Tanbou is not "popular" media. And yet, by its journalistic practices, by the way the radio hosts and journalists position themselves in relation to the listeners through their media discourse, by the way the station operates in relation to the public, Radyo Tanbou constructs an ideological position which reflects the tensions underlying the complex network of cultural relationships in Guadeloupe, much more effectively than any other outlet in the country.

Ideological Position

What is this ideological position and how is it constructed? First of all, what seems clear is that the station defines its position by using certain journalistic strategies to establish a close personal relationship with its listeners.

The station allots time to its program schedule to all organized sectors of society; youth, social, professional, and immigrant groups, and union movements. Journalists seek out the opinions of the listening public on all matters; they encourage listeners to phone in and to report injustices, thus transforming the listening public into individuals who suddenly have status as potential colleagues and free-lance investigative journalists (Interview, Mekel Barbotteau, 1987).

As well, the public is invited to visit the station and at times children even come in for help with their homework. This openness creates a feeling of trust, confidence, and credibility—feelings one finds in a close-knit family relationship.

What interests us for the moment is the nature of this collective family voice and the way it is framed by the voice speaking on the radio. In all news reports, interviews, and discussions with invited guests, the journalists and hosts make clear distinctions between "we" and "they." "They" can be loosely defined as the "colonial forces," all institutions and individuals who accept and work openly to consolidate the departmental relationship. "They" are not ignored or transformed into an abstract mass because "they" are interviewed and "they" take part in discussions as members of political parties, as visiting Metropolitan dignitaries, as local businessmen, and polticians. However, once these voices are on the air, they become part of the ideological construct of the station, because they are placed in their appropriate ideological space by the journalist, who, through his or her choice of pronouns, distinguishes the "others" from those with which we, the listeners are supposed to sympathize.

At the same time, the journalist or host always associates himself/ herself with the sympathetic listening group—understood as the Guadeloupean people: "our word" (pawol an-nou), "our country" (péyi an-nou), "our strength" (fos an-nou), "we have a role to play" (nous avons un rôle à jouer), "we have a common cause" (nous avons une cause commune), "that should make us think" (cela devrait nous faire réfléchir)[2]. Because the journalist shares his voice with the collective listening voice, he also shares his act of speaking. When he names, asks, questions, criticizes, and establishes an ideological space through this voice, the listeners themselves are also symbolically taking part in this dialogue, expressing themselves and in so doing, constructing their own collective subject position through the voice speaking on the radio.

This collective subject has specific characteristics which are defined by the information content. It confirms its Caribbean cultural identity by rejecting expressions of the French national culture. This means it recognizes the ideological function of the imposition of a national language, so it talks Creole and refuses to talk French. It refuses a homogeneous national culture of European origin and affirms itself as a culturally syncretic subject by emphasizing the traditions of the various ethnic groups which make up the population of the island: East Indian, Middle Eastern, African, and European.

This collective subject has a strong geo-political identity within the sphere of the Americas, rather than in the east-west relation with Europe and Metropolitan France. A detailed analysis of the news content reveals that internal news coverage deals mostly with local issues that do not involve the Metropolitan society, and the external news gives an important place to the Caribbean countries and Latin America. Instead of using segments of news reports sent in from the Metropolitan news sources, such as Europe 1 or France-Inter, the station relies on local correspondents and Caribbean sources such as CANA (Caribbean News Agency), *Eastern Caribbean News*, and *Caribbean Contact* from Barbados. As well, Radio— Canada, Die Deutsche Welle, and the BBC are monitored from Radio Antilles in Montserrat, and when money is available, their local journalists travel to different parts of the Caribbean to cover important events. For example, Radyo Tanbou was the only local station to have a journalist in Haïti reporting directly on the departure of Duvalier.

By making its radio voices close associates of its listeners, Radyo Tanbou is perceived as recognizing the value of the indigenous cultural reality and as consolidating close ties with the surrounding Caribbean countries. The voices are perceived as willing to express criticism and raise questions in the face of a clearly-identified opposition. Securely entrenched in a well defined family space where "Rico," "Ernestin," "Julien," and other members of the "family" attend to each other's needs, the voices produce an extremely seductive and reassuring subject position.

Notwithstanding this tendency to place themselves within the family of listeners, the voices of Radyo Tanbou also establish themselves as independent subjects, speaking from a position outside the group.

One example of this appeared during a discussion on the Sunday morning talk show, "What have you got to say about that?" ("Kaw ka di de sa?") The discussion revolved around the law of "l'Europe unique," which will make Guadeloupe part of the European Common Market in 1992. A caller, frustrated that there was no way of knowing public opinion on this matter, wanted Radyo Tanbou to conduct a poll, announce the results, and then hold a forum to help decide what collective protest actions should be taken (assuming the result would be negative.) Nothing was actually done, but the fact that the caller perceived the station as a focal point for collective action and a force which could arbitrate differences of opinion, indicates that not only does the Radyo Tanbou voice inspire trust and confidence, but also that it is perceived as speaking from a neutral space from where it can transcend internal differences and resolve contradictions. This double role of the journalist as a voice operating within the group and above the group has interesting consequences.

The radio voice announces meetings, demonstrations, gatherings concerning political prisoners and these events are often broadcast. When controversies arise, such as the recent increase in the municipal tax in the commune of Moule, all sides of the debate are allowed air time. In this particular instance, the mayor, the council members, as well as spokespeople for the opposition, and representatives of local taxpayers, were invited to provide arguments showing that finances had or had not been mismanaged.[3] This sense of what is perceived as fairplay produces a friendly radio space.

The radio voice also places itself in an external position by intervening through other discursive strategies. An example of this was provided by the same program "Kaw ka di de sa." The difficult relationship between the Socialist Party (Parti socialiste) and the Federation of the Socialist Party of Guadeloupe (Fédération du Parti socialiste de la Guadeloupe) was being discussed. The conversation ended with a series of comments by the host, leading the listener, step by step, to adopt the host's point of view. First, the radio host confirmed the essentially tolerant and open nature of Radyo Tanbou, because it encourages the expression of opposing opinions. He then positioned himself outside the debate by disqualifying both opinions, because they did not address the fundamental problem in the country, which is the moral and political legitimacy of overseas departments.

The journalist establishes his overriding authority here by assuming a didactic function; he reformulates the arguments, simplifies the reasoning, and brings out the essential ideas in order to put the whole discussion in an easily understandable form. Then, he moves on to a more subtle reasoning by pointing out the egocentric political ambitions of a few individuals against the broader common interests which can only be understood in ideological, not political, terms, says the host. Political discussions, concerned with party platforms and policy questions, do not address the basic assumption that the present system is wrong. It is obvious that what the speaker is trying to do is not guide the specific political choices but rather mold a whole system of beliefs.

This kind of discourse, while it is manipulative, is effective, because it addresses all levels of the listening public, from the least educated to the most politically sophisticated. Thus, it tends to bypass class and political differences, discourage devisive thinking, and produce an homogenous ideological position, which transforms itself into the close-knit family relationship that they hope will carry the population towards its ultimate common goal.

The journalists use such discursive mechanisms as the irrefutable rhetorical question: "What you are really saying here is why not encourage economic development in our own country?"; (News bulletin, 5 January 1988) "Are we ready for change...Can we build something new?" "Is it good enough to say I am not happy?" ("Kaw ka di de sa?" Radyo Tanbou, 21 February 1988). These questions eventually become critical affirmations: "We have a media system which puts Guadeloupeans to sleep, which makes them passive. We have to resist that." "Elected representatives should make more effort to change things."

Ultimately, this pedagogical strategy is meant to stimulate critical thinking. By asking questions which presuppose the answer, by making statements that draw the original subject matter into the larger question of the legitimacy of the present system, the Radyo Tanbou voice becomes a provocation which forces the listener to remain intellectually active.

At this point, one obvious question comes to mind. How is it that such a radio station is authorized to continue broadcasting? One might be tempted to describe France as an enlightened democracy which tolerates all extremes, but recent events in New Caledonia tend to refute that.

The answer seems to lie squarely on the shoulders of Radyo Tanbou itself. It shows it is well aware of the limits of state tolerance, because it instigates a self-imposed censorship which functions in one very obvious way. While this collective "we" does ask embarrassing questions, while it does broadcast events which other stations do not air because of their controversial or "delicate" political nature, while it does offer resistance by questioning power relations, protesting openly, and proclaiming the need for change, Radyo Tanbou does not advocate violence. In fact, it does not propose any concrete acts of any kind.

These are obviously media, as well as political, strategies, but solutions are inevitably presented in terms that are either very general or abstract. For example, the journalists say: "We have to act. (...) We have a media system which puts Guadeloupeans to sleep, which makes them passive; we have to resist that. (...) Elected representatives should make more effort to change things;" We have to "win the victory;" We have to "decide for ourselves;" "We have to reflect on this problem so that we can progress in a more lucid fashion" (Il faut réfléchir sur ce problème pour nous permettre d'avancer avec plus de lucidité); everyone must "look at things as they are and not get carried away by passion" (regarder en face et dépasser les passions inutiles).

Not only do they not advocate violence, but by inviting points of view from all political parties and movements, by taking grassroots protest seriously and providing a public forum for anger and frustration, Radyo Tanbou also serves as an important channel for defusing potential violence by allowing nationalist ideas to circulate freely. Might one argue then, that the station also functions as a conservative force, because it directs this protest into channels tightly controlled by a trusted voice, and, thus, it prevents the protesting subject from endangering the stability and the security of the general structure of things? By not posing an immediate threat to the existing system, but by presenting, through language, a counter ideology which deconstructs the homogenous subject imposed on the public by years of exposure to cultural practices that reflect the national ideology of Metropolitan France, Radyo Tanbou insures the continued flow of an opposing stream of cultural attitudes that can assert itself with great confidence on the airwaves. Thus, this radio station confirms its function as a particular instance of media technology which has become a serious outlet for popular discontent.

Appendix

Summary of Morning News Bulletins

RFO (Radio France Outre mer)
13h00, Friday, 8 January, 1988
Fifteen minutes of international news followed by five minutes of regional news.
Source: France—Inter via satellite from France and local journalists.

Regional News:
> Announcement of a new lottery game in the French overseas departments.
> Strike by Air France workers in Pointe-á-Pitre.
> Changes in the system of paid parking in the Airport of Guadeloupe.
> The Crédit Foncier of France has created a single outlet for building loans.
> The Grand Master of the Masonic Lodge of France is in Guadeloupe.

Radyo Tanbou
12h30, Tuesday, 5 January 1988.
Thirty minutes.
Source: local journalists
News Items:
> In depth report concerning the eventual entry of Guadeloupe in the European Economic Community in 1992. Discussion about the movement of multinational companies and the work force. Interview with the Customs commissioner who doesn't see how customs will function under the act.
> Discussion about the mobilization of the population of Le Moule to protest the municipal tax increase. Founding of the "Mouvement populaire pour la défense des intérêts des contribuables mouliens." Interview with the president of this organization and others protesting the increase.
> Discussion of the activities of the Chamber of Commerce of Small Business and Craftsmen: areas of development, problems caused by moonlighting.
> Questions raised by the journalist concerning a decision by the "Conseil général" to allow a department store in Abymes to expand its surface. Questions were raised as to the way the final vote was interpreted and the possibility that some of the council members knew what the outcome of the vote would be.
> Discussion with a representative of ACUPEL (Association coopérative pour des produits de l'élevage) concerning their association with the Chamber of Commerce. Problems concerning the marketing of meat products: butchers, slaughter house, retail sale points. Journalist proposes a synthesis, emphasizing that what is really being said here is that Guadeloupeans must encourage economic development in their own country.

RCI (Radio Caríbes international)
13h00, Friday, 8 January 1988.
Sixteen minutes, mixed bulletin of French and regional news.
Source: Europe 1 via satellite and local journalists

News Items:

Report on the new immigration policy.

Report on the financial problems of the Parisian daily *Le Matin*.

Report on the Crédit Agricole, a French financial institution.

Announcement of a debate held in Trois Rivières (Guadeloupe) on agricultural development.

Report on the Paris—Dakar car rally.

French government refuses to allow a football player from Paraguay to play on a French team.

Discussion about the problem of drugs in France.

Report on the popularity of the "Rolling Stones.

Interview with a local dance teacher about the upcoming show at the Art Centre (Pointe—à—Pitre) with dancers from the Paris Opera Ballet.

Chapter Ten
Grassroots Basketball in Trinidad and Tobago:
Foreign Domination or Local Creativity*

Joan D. Mandle
and
Jay R. Mandle

Introduction

In Trinidad and Tobago, numerous organized basketball leagues involve thousands of adult men and women. Our study concerns the reasons for this active grassroots participation. In particular, we ask whether, and the extent to which, basketball should be understood as a cultural imposition on the people of Trinidad and Tobago. Alternatively, we investigate whether the sport's popularity represents an activity which, though imported, has taken root in the country and has become an arena in which local basketballers express their creativity and skill.

The literature dealing with the spread of sport from developed to less developed countries overwhelmingly emphasizes the derivative nature of much sport activity in the poor countries. It points to sport as a heretofore unexamined domain of cultural dependency. For example, Henning Eichberg views the diffusion of sport from metropolitan to Third World countries as "superimposed by colonial and neocolonial pressures." According to Eichberg, the relationship between underdeveloped and developed countries is one of "economic dominance and neocolonization by Western capitalism in sport as in other areas (Eichberg 1984: 97-105). Similarly, Richard Gruneau's recent work includes a discussion of the "asymmetrical" and dependent relationship between developed and less developed countries with respect to sport activity. He argues that international sport, exemplified by the Olympic games, represents "little sharing of cultures," but rather offers only the "institutionalized agonistic activities that developed in the western

*This chapter is based in part on material from *Grass Roots Commitment: Basketball and Society in Trinidad and Tebago*, Caribbean Books, 1988. Available from Box H, Parkersburg, IA 50665.

capitalist nations and were spread through the colonial networks of those nations" (Gruneau 1983: 173). Both scholars, then, view the diffusion of sport as part of a more general pattern of economic, social, and cultural imperialism which creates and reflects periphery dependency and metropolitan domination.

A different view of the North to South diffusion of sport sees Northern dominance in a less hostile light. This approach suggests that sport spreads because Third World people take developed countries as their model, and seek to emulate them. Allen Guttman, for example, writes that the acceptance of baseball in countries such as the Dominican Republic, Venezuela, and Puerto Rico indicates that the people there are "strongly and favorably impressed with the U.S. as a model of modern civilization" (Guttman, 1978). This view also identifies the primacy of the role of the metropolitan power in explaining the diffusion of sport. Here, however, culture is not imposed. Rather, the people of the Third World respond to, and attempt to imitate the culture of developed countries in the form of the sports they play. In both approaches, domination by developed countries means that the people of underdeveloped societies are vested with little choice and/or creativity with respect to the sport activities in which they participate. Like world systems and dependency theory, there is a tendency in this literature to see external factors, emanating from the developed countries, as the most important or even the only determinant of sport participation in the Third World (Wallerstein 1974-80).

A dissenter from this paradigm is Frank Manning. Even Manning, however, in his study of local sport and sport clubs in Bermuda, at first accepted the dependency perspective. He indicates that his initial hypothesis, developed prior to his actual field work, was that "Bermudian society was an imitative version of that exemplified by the tourist" (Manning 1973: 261). He expected to find that sport and club behavior among Bermudians were simply a reflection of the lifestyle and behavior of tourists visiting Bermuda from developed countries. Manning's careful ethnographic field work on sport clubs, however, convinced him of the inadequacy of that perspective. As he writes, the "Bermudian response to tourist influences was more complex and more oriented toward the indigenous culture than is generally assumed" (Manning 1973: 261). Manning does not deny the pervasive influence of metropolitan cultures, and especially in the case of Bermuda, of tourism. But his work, nonetheless, argues persuasively for the importance of factors specific to the indigenous culture and social structure as the central determinants in the development and organization of sport and gaming behavior in that country.

Basketball in Trinidad and Tobago

The issue of dependency versus the salience of local conditions in the adoption of culture is particularly relevant in a case study of basketball in Trinidad and Tobago. Our investigation is based on participant observation of grassroots basketball teams and leagues throughout the country at various times over a four year period, as well as with interviews with former basketball organizers and players, and with newspaper reporters covering sports in the country.

An examination of basketball's history in Trinidad and Tobago leaves no doubt that the United States played an important role in the sport's adoption. The game was first played in Trinidad among the Chinese and Lebanese ethnic populations during the 1930s, but its play did not spread from these tiny enclaves to large numbers of the population. It was not until World War II that basketball began to take hold in Trinidad and Tobago. During the war, American troops were stationed at Chaguaramus, a military base about five miles west of the capital city, Port of Spain. These American soldiers are reported to have played basketball among themselves and with Trinidadians, both at a gymnasium on the base and at a nearby recreational facility, the Woodbrook Center. During this period, seven or eight Trinidadian teams were organized, including a team associated with the Trinidad Defense Force, all of which played one another and the Americans. The games drew both interest and crowds, and, soon after, a Trinidad team began to participate in international competition. One informant—a sports writer for a local paper—even referred to the early 1950s as the "heyday of basketball in Trinidad."

A second important and more recent American influence on the growth of basketball stems from the increasing opportunity of Trinidadians and Tobagonians to view American professional basketball games on television or on videotapes. The taped retelecasting of National Basketball Association (NBA) games by Trinidad and Tobago Television (TTT), the local television outlet, was a frequent occurrence by the 1980s. The potentially-powerful nature of this influence is suggested by the fact that television receiver ownership in Trinidad and Tobago is remarkably extensive. According to UNESCO, the number of television sets per 1,000 inhabitants in Trinidad and Tobago is higher than any South American country, and ranks below only the U.S., Canada, Bermuda, the United States Virgin Islands, and Puerto Rico in the Western Hemisphere (UNESCO 1985: Table 10: 4). More recently the spread of videocassette recorders and the direct telecast of NBA games by satellite have further increased the opportunity to watch professional basketball. Many of our basketballer informants reported "watching every [basketball] game on Saturday afternoons during the season." Viewing professional basketball on television is important to Trinidad and Tobago basketballers. Indeed one player—a Tobagonian woman named Pearl—

expressed great concern about our access to a television set. (All names are fictitious to protect anonymity). She repeatedly asked us if we had the use of a TV, and was greatly relieved to learn that we did, explaining, "I wouldn't want you to miss the NBA game that will be on TV this Saturday. Everyone will be watching it." This same athlete proudly, though perhaps with some exaggeration, told us that she had watched "every single game the 76ers played." Tom, a player from the Trinidad neighborhood of Laventille, further attested to the important influence of televised basketball games. He told us:

On Saturday afternoon when there is an NBA game playing, you never see anyone at the [basketball] courts. Then when the game is over, you'll see maybe one, then another and another people coming from their houses to the courts to try to practice what they see the NBA players doing.

Knowledge of and interest in the NBA is evident in other ways as well. Basketballers know a great deal about NBA teams and about individual NBA players, and they discourse at length on their strengths and weaknesses. The NBA playoffs, underway at the time of our 1986 field research, were a subject of much interest. Sitting in the stand watching a basketball game in Tobago, we listened while spectators engaged in animated arguments concerning which NBA team would win the playoffs. Their detailed knowledge of NBA players and teams was impressive. The skills of individual players were commented on and evaluated, as well as the differing abilities of teams. One after another, basketballers asserted with great intensity their conviction that their favorite team would be victorious.

NBA influence is evident also in the nicknames which players give one another, and in the names of the teams playing in Trinidad and Tobago leagues. The names of NBA stars are frequently employed as nicknames by local players. We heard players referred to as "Michael Jordan," "Sidney Moncreif," and other NBA stars. Not just individuals, but often team names reflect NBA or U.S. influences. For example, the Laventille League includes teams named the "Rockets," "Celtics," "Lakers," and "Knicks"— each a counterpart to the name of a professional team in the U.S.—as well as a "Pittsburgh" team named for that U.S. city.

The style of the basketball played in Trinidad and Tobago also seems to suggest the influence of the NBA. Many basketballers in the country try to develop spectacular individual offensive moves, seemingly modeled on those employed by NBA players. Illustrative of this was an impromptu "slam dunk" contest, organized one evening in Trinidad after a game had been rained out. As each player drove to the basket in turn, trying to "dunk" the ball, he would call out the name of a NBA star famous for his "slam dunk" ability. Bystanders joined in, exclaiming, "Here comes 'Dr. J'," or shouting the name of other NBA stars, as players approached the basket. This celebration of individual skills continued into the evening, even though few successful "dunks" were actually executed. Great enthusiasm was generated by the small but vociferous crowd which gathered to cheer these attempts to replicate the "slams" they had observed NBA players perform. Thus, the impact of NBA players as models—especially in the development of basketball skills—seems beyond question. This appreciation of individual offensive skills—especially "dunks"—was also evident in league games. In Point Fortin, for example, a successful "dunk" in a big game one evening sent the crowd into a frenzy, and brought all the player's teammates, and not a few spectators, onto the middle of the court to offer "high fives."

Over and above "slam dunks," the influence of the U.S. professional sport on skills development is patent. Many Trinidadian and Tobagonians can, with ease, dribble behind their backs or between their legs. In this, there seems to be a clear reflection of the ball-handling dexterity of the NBA point guards. A considerable number of Trinidadian and Tobagonian players know how to "pump fake," in order to place their defensive counterparts at a disadvantage. And they also know the value of playing the game above the level of the basket in order to obtain maximum offensive efficiency.

The importance of the NBA can be seen in other, perhaps more unexpected ways. We noticed, for example, that the recently resurfaced Laventille basketball court had lane markings which were different from other Trinidad and Tobago courts. Laventille's configuration did not conform to International Amateur Basketball Federation (FIBA) rules, which govern basketball in the country. When asked for an explanation of this anomaly, the president of the Laventille league affirmed that his executive committee had decided to paint the courts according to NBA rules. It did so, he told us, hoping to encourage local teams to play "like in the NBA games because they are so exciting." He asserted that basketball in Trinidad and Tobago would be helped by making it more similar to NBA games because, "Then more people would come out for the games."

Emphasis on Individualism

In Trinidad and Tobago, basketball is played in the rhythms and patterns associated with individual, rather than team, basketball. Because of this, and in spite of highly-developed individual skills, basketball in the country exhibits serious weaknesses. In the many games we observed, tenacious defense was rarely played. Typically a zone defense was employed, but players engaged in very little truly aggressive effort to prevent the offense from scoring. Similarly, patterned basketball was only rarely seen on offense. "Off the ball" or "weak-side" screening was infrequently used. A limited number of set plays could be seen, but offensive basketball much more involved a series of "one on one" moves, or individual fast breaks to the basket, than a team concept, in which the individual skills of the players were combined into a cooperative effort.

The problem with this is that one style of play is not, in fact, as good as another, for in sport, a universal standard of achievement is present. Participants in competitive sports are evaluated primarily by their ability to be victorious. In basketball, a more orchestrated, cooperative team of players will almost always defeat a comparably skilled group of individualists who do not play as a cohesive unit. As a result, the almost exclusively individual style of play we observed in Trinidad and Tobago represents a lower standard than could otherwise be achieved. Furthermore, the lack of cooperative team play and the consequent relative weakness in the sport is widely recognized and bemoaned by the basketballers themselves. One informant, for example, lamented what he referred to as the "stupidity" of individual play, complaining that teams did not "set up or run plays which were sure to score." In another instance, we overheard a basketballer repeating over and over again, as he watched players attempting to execute difficult individual moves in lieu of cooperative play during a league game, "Exhibitionism, exhibitionism. That's what ruins basketball in Trinidad and Tobago."

In addition to the desire to imitate the skills of specific NBA players, there are several other possible sources of this emphasis on individual skills. It is likely that the lack of coaching in basketball communities is at least part of the problem. Most coaches in the leagues have had no formal training in playing or coaching basketball, simply picking up their skills, like most players, informally. In addition, in most cases their involvement with basketball began only when they were well into their teenage years. One informant told us that virtually no Trinidadians or Tobagonians play basketball before they are seventeen or eighteen years old. Prior to that, in school and in informal leagues, they play other sports, particularly football. Basketball is played almost exclusively by mature players, who have had no prior coaching or training in the game. The players who are willing to serve as coaches, thus, have no long-term grounding in the sport, and have themselves rarely been coached.

This situation results in a low level of coaching in Trinidad and Tobago. On the one hand, most coaches do not have enough knowledge to teach either sophisticated offensive or defensive play. On the other hand, as contemporaries of their fellow players, they often have difficulty in exercising authority. They frequently are unable to insist on training, or on a disciplined pattern of team play. As one Trinidadian coach recounted, "I tell my players to pass the ball and to get back to play defense, but they never listen." In general, the weakness in coaching is undoubtedly one factor accounting for the fact that team basketball is rarely observed, and that games frequently are a showcase only for individual skills.

The emphasis on individual, rather than team, play may also have another source, one stemming from the influence of television as a major mechanism of basketball's diffusion to Trinidad and Tobago. What is transmitted on the television screen is only a partial representation of the actual play of the game. Typically, the television camera focuses narrowly on the movement of the basketball, and rivets attention to the actions of the player with the ball. But much of the success in playing basketball, both offensively and defensively, is determined by actions undertaken by players who do not have the ball, and are not in the vicinity of the ball, but who nonetheless engage in cooperative movements with each other. Both the importance and the manner of the execution of the fundamentals of the sport are insufficiently highlighted in televised basketball. As a result, it is likely that there is a significant skewing in the skills which are learned when the principal exposure to the game is the video screen.

The individual skills seen by Trinidadians and Tobagonians on television are also defined by the fact that these telecasts are those of NBA players. Thus, not only does television highlight individual skills, but also those on display are executed by the most talented individual basketball players in the world. The fact that the camera tends to underline individual skills, and that the players on display are those with consummate personal competencies, produces an emphasis on individual, rather than team, play. Referring to the lack of a team style game in Trinidad and Tobago, Clive, himself a player/coach, shook his head in disgust, saying that watching NBA stars on TV teaches individual moves, but "not really how to play basketball."

One other possible explanation for the preponderance of individual, rather than team, skills must be mentioned, although we have little data by which to evaluate this hypothesis. Axthelm and others, who have examined the basketball played in the streets of black low-income urban neighborhoods in the U.S., have reported the dominance of spectacular and expressive play by individual players, play which seems similar to that which we have observed (Axthelm 1971). Their explanation for this emphasis on individual, rather than team, play includes both social structural and cultural variables.

On the one hand, it is suggested that low income individuals, at the bottom of a hierarchical class system, see in basketball play one of the few areas where they can demonstrate their individual self-worth and achievement. In such a situation, individuals may use uniquely creative moves on the basketball court as a much-needed opportunity for self-expression. The individualist—even flamboyant—style of play, though perhaps contrary to the requirements of effective team basketball, may nonetheless fulfill social and psychic needs on an individual level. An alternative explanation emphasizes cultural factors as the source of stylized play on the basketball court. It has been suggested that Black culture strongly values creative, expressive behavior. Whether, as some have suggested, the sources of this expressive behavior lie in aspects of an indigenous African culture which have been retained in the Americas, or whether individual innovation and embellishment have emerged as a hallmark of Black culture in North America and the Caribbean, subsequent to the diaspora, is not clear (Stuckey 1987). Either as representing continuity with African culture, or as the development of a new aesthetic in the Western hemisphere, it may be that Black culture rewards individual expressive play and thus shapes the style of basketball typically played by Blacks, whether in the U.S. or Caribbean.

Unfortunately, the data we generated in observing Trinidad and Tobago basketball are not adequate to provide insight into these last issues: the extent to which or whether the sport's individual style is consonant with African culture in continuity, or whether it allows for expression of a New World Black sensibility associated with social class and social structure. While it would be fascinating to pursue this question with a comparative study of, for example, Caribbean and West African basketball, such an enterprise is beyond our current scope.

What our data do allow us conclude is that Trinidad and Tobago basketball is profoundly shaped both by the locus of origin of the sport—the U.S.—and also by the means by which it was transferred and absorbed in Trinidad and Tobago. Once basketball was introduced by U.S. soldiers, its specific configuration was influenced by the fact that Trinidadians and Tobagonians were exposed to professional U.S. basketball via television. This, in conjunction with the fact that little indigenous coaching was available, meant that much of the specific content of the game clearly was influenced by the way basketball is played at the highest level in the U.S.

No Imperialism

Despite the obvious importance of U.S. basketball in the origins and growth of the sport in Trinidad and Tobago, the role of the U.S. was never volunteered as an explanation when we queried basketballers on this subject. No one cited, for example, admiration for the U.S. or its culture in explaining why the sport was popular, or why he/she played it. Neither did anyone indicate that basketball was imposed on them by the U.S. Indeed one informant, Carlisle, vehemently denied that external factors, such as identification with or interest in NBA stars, were of importance in explaining why Trinidadians and Tobagonians played basketball. He said, "Sure we watch the NBA, but that is not enough for us to want to play the game or for it to become so popular." He agreed that Trinidadians and Tobagonians had, in part, learned how to play by watching Americans. But at the same time, he discounted this external influence as an explanation of why they played the game. On the contrary, Carlisle and other basketballers emphasized the importance of motivating factors within Trinidad and Tobago itself.

The three most frequently mentioned responses to the question of why basketballers play the game were its inexpensive character, its accessibility, and its action. Many informants mentioned that "basketball doesn't cost much." For individuals to play basketball informally, neither a great deal of equipment nor large expenditures on their part are necessary. As one player said with a grin, "All you need is a pair of sneaks, a ball and a ring." That a well built and lighted court is preferable was affirmed by the president of the Tobago league, when he commented that basketball spreads most quickly if good courts and facilities are provided. Nonetheless, improvised and inexpensive facilities often are sufficient to nurture and sustain individual interest in the game.

Accessibility means that the facilities necessary to play basketball are readily available to players. One basketballer, Cleon, told us that he liked basketball much better than football or cricket (the two most popular Caribbean sports) because "You have to walk all the way to the savannah to play them, but basketball is right on my own street. All I have to do is roll out of bed to play." Basketball is also more accessible because it requires fewer players. It can be played with just two players or with ten. As one basketballer said, "Basketball is always right there and you only need one other person to sweat."

In discussing his youth in the capital city of Port of Spain, another player, Tom, emphasized accessibility, describing how, when he was a young man, he could stop almost anywhere for a pick-up game in the evening on his way to another activity: "Even if I was dressed to go out, I could always play a couple of quick games and then dry off in the breeze." A sports writer for a local newspaper recounted that in the 1960s, "Everyone was putting up a ring in their yard. Basketball was everywhere." We found that people had made basketball accessible even in remote villages. During a drive through the hills of Tobago, we came upon the tiny village of Bethel, perched alone on the top of a mountain in the center of the island. The village boasts a community center with a basketball court. But equally symbolic to us was the fact that, as we drove along, we came upon three eight-year old boys shooting baskets at an old hoop which had been nailed to a tree by the road. From our vantage point, we could see the island spread before us, and hear nothing but a tethered cow chewing her cud and the sound of a bouncing basketball.

It is also the drama and action of basketball that is appealing. One Tobagonian woman, whose brothers and husband had all played basketball, reported enjoying the games because, "They are exciting and full of action." Other players indicated that they "love to sweat," stressing the exertion that basketball necessitates. Spectators in the small town of Point Fortin, many of whom crowded onto court to watch league play night after night, cited its quick action and excitement as central reasons for their intense interest in the sport.

The excitement, inexpensive nature, and accessibility of basketball clearly are important aspects of the game's popularity. However, the appeal of the game is not confined to that of a casual, though enjoyable, activity. For many Trinidadians and Tobagonians, participation in basketball's play and administration fills a uniquely meaningful role in their lives. This is because basketball is a sport which is primarily organized by the players themselves. It is their game: from the pick-up street corner action to the highly complex system of leagues in the country. Indeed, for many players, basketball is the central organizing focus of their lives. Frequently we heard players say, "I don't know what I would do without basketball," or "It is the most important thing in my life." A Tobagonian woman player, Nora, described how, although she had enjoyed the opportunity to go to Italy for three months as a member of steel band, "I almost went crazy because I couldn't play basketball."

One player described to us the importance of basketball in his life. John grew up in the slums of Port of Spain, in one of the poorest and, in his words, "baddest" sections of the capital city. In his neighborhood, basketball was very popular and John played frequently. As he grew older and left school, John's life took on the pattern of many young poor Trinidadians. He described himself as "heavily into drugs of all kinds and out of work most of the time," as well as involved in petty illegal activities. Mostly he "hung on the streets with the other guys." During this period, he said "Basketball was my life line." He would play and "train," no matter what else was happening. He said he and his friends "lived on the court...we had nothing else to do." As he describes it, basketball was the focus of his life, the "only thing that got me through in those years." For many young Trinidadians and Tobagonians whose live are similar to that of John, basketball constitutes an important—even central—structural focus on their lives (also see Blanchard 1981).

Trinidadian and Tobagonian basketballers are profoundly serious about their sport. League games are played at numerous locations throughout the country. At many games, particularly on Friday and

Saturday evenings, or when killer games are scheduled, attendance is substantial, and the pitch of excitement high. Only very rarely did we observe games played at less than a serious level of intensity. In games played at the highest level of competition or in games of significance to league standings, the emotional involvement which we observed is comparable to that of intercollegiate or professional games played in the U.S.

Basketball is important not only because the basketballers spend a great deal of time and energy on it but because it is theirs—it constitutes a community in which they initiate and influence what goes on. They play it, coach it, referee it, and run the leagues. Basketball is where they belong, where they feel comfortable, and where they can be valued and appreciated for their skills and contribution, as players, coaches, referees, or organizers and administrators. Basketball is thus an arena—chosen by the participants—where they can express themselves, where they can exercise some degree of control, and which has important personal and social meaning to them.

Participation in basketball is intensely important to members of the basketball communities because it resonates with their own needs and competencies. No one forces the Trinidad and Tobago basketballers to play the game; nor do they do so in order to pattern themselves after the U.S. Even their enormous interest in the NBA seems more to reflect their desire to raise their own performance to a high standard, than simply adoration or mimicry (Naipaul 1969).

In Trinidad and Tobago, basketballers generally are low income individuals: it is a game played by the materially deprived. As noted earlier, we cannot know whether their low income status affects the specific style of the basketball played in the country. However, it does seem clear that their relative poverty is a factor which is important in understanding why they actively participate in basketball communities. Ranking at the bottom of a class-stratified society, they suffer from the lack of power and control associated with that status. Alienated from influence in mainstream society, their participation in basketball—being part of a committed and ongoing community—may represent a way partly to counter the feelings associated with that estrangement. This is because actively helping to shape an important activity in an on-going community, as well as playing and mastering the skills associated with a sport, are empowering activities (Anderson 1976). Further, participation in basketball represents a way in which individuals and groups can test and extend the limits of their own performance. In doing that, the exhilarating experience of victory can become a benchmark by which to assess their achievement, and, in that way, demonstrate accomplishment.

In light of the profundity of the grassroots commitment to basketball, it seems clearly inaccurate to see the sport primarily as an external imposition or as testimony to some other society's virtues. It is true that West Indians have long been exposed to, and influenced by, external cultural patterns: first, those of the colonial power that controlled these islands; more recently, those of the U.S. through its dominance in the region and its ubiquitous media presence.

Rather than merely a manifestation of cultural imperialism, in which West Indians simply are acted upon by powerful external forces, we believe that a dialectic relationship is present in basketball. The diffusion of the sport does reflect the reality of dominance and subordination between the cultures of the U.S. and Trinidad and Tobago. Culture forms do flow from North to South and primarily not vice versa; basketball is part of this traffic. But basketball in Trinidad and Tobago does not remain foreign. It becomes indigenized by a section of the population who sees in it a vehicle to create meaning in their lives. For these people, basketball—both its play and organization—becomes an important outlet. As such, it represents a realm of freedom and creativity, a form of their own cultural articulation, and this despite basketball's foreign origins.

Obviously basketball was learned from Americans, and this U.S. influence is reinforced by telecasts from the U.S. In addition, American professional basketball influences the style of play in Trinidad and Tobago. In that sense, it clearly is part of the process of North to South cultural diffusion. But this fact is not, in and of itself, of much significance in explaining why Trinidadians and Tobagonians play the game. Culture is cosmopolitan; its spread is commonplace. What is important is not where a cultural form originated, but what happens to it upon its arrival. The issue of significance is whether it remains alien in content and form, dependent upon external patronage for its continuation, or whether it takes hold in a way so that it becomes indigenous and creatively integrated into the lives of the local population.

The region's historical context of colonialism, and its geographic proximity to the U.S., has resulted in its vulnerability to cultural imperialism. The development of an indigenous West Indian culture has, as a result, been impeded. Nonetheless, there has been, and still is, room for cultural expressiveness and creative choice on the part of people (Genovese, 1974). In the current circumstances, there can be no doubt that the impact of contact with some forms of foreign culture is stifling and harmful. But contact with foreign culture, as in the case of basketball, may on the contrary, provide the Caribbean people—even the most deprived among them—with the opportunity to engage in new patterns of activities and organization which satisfy their own needs, and which become fulfilling and creative forms of expression.

Notes

Chapter One

[1]See at least 27 February, 19 June 1983; 5 August 1984; 19 May, 9 June, 14 July, 22 September, 27 October 1985; 15 June, 22 June, 21 September, 28 September, 2 November 1986; 22 February, 19 April, 7 June, 5 July, 13 September 1987, and 31 January 1988.

Chapter Two

This article is published simultaneously in *Plantation Society*, Vol III (1990). The author is grateful to Thomas Fiehrer and John Lent for their cooperation in facilitating this arrangement.

[1]There is considerable variation between these festivals, and "purists" might argue that two of them—the Washington and Hartford events—are better described as generalized Caribbean celebrations than as carnivals. The others belong unquestionably to the carnival genre.

[2]Montreal is an exception, as it had an appreciable black population before the current flow of Caribbean immigrants. Otherwise, black Canadians of older standing are settled largely in Nova Scotia and in rural areas of southwestern Ontario.

[3]It is not, perhaps, coincidental that a British scholar, Richard Burton (1985), has done the outstanding work in exploring the symbolic and social historical affinities between cricket and Carnival.

Chapter Three

[1]Fieldwork was supported by grants from the University of Illinois, Department of Anthropology, and the University of Illinois Graduate College.

Chapter Four

[1]The presence of "bamboula" dancers points to the Trinidad influence in the Virgin Islands Carnival. Andrew Pearse (1971), in his article on Carnival in nineteenth century Trinidad, writes that it was common for whites to dress as slaves and dance the "bamboula," "giouba," and "calinda."

[2]In 1950, whites constituted 3.1 percent of St. John's population. By 1980, they accounted for 26.3 percent of the population, and, in 1987, the white percentage was estimated at 31 percent.

Chapter Five

[1]The director of ICYC is Dr. Deanna Robinson of the University of Oregon. The group has a book forthcoming with Sage Publications authored by Deanna Robinson, Elizabeth Buck and Marlene Cuthbert, and will be publishing a case study volume as well. The authors are grateful to ICYC for permission to use the data.

[2]Unless otherwise indicated, interviews referred to in this section were conducted in 1987, by Gladstone Wilson, Kingston, Jamaica, while he was an M.A. candidate in communication studies at the University of Windsor.

[3]The interview was for a study conducted by Marlene Cuthbert, "Cultural Autonomy and Popular Music: A Survey of Jamaican Youth" in *Communication Research* 12:3 (July 1985), pp. 381-93.

[4]Tavares-Finson,Tom. "Current Status of Copyright Legislation in Jamaica," interview with Heather Royes, *Jamaica Journal*, 1983, p. 15 and Beverley Pereira, "Copyright in Jamaica," *JLA Bulletin* 1985/86, p. 36.

[5]Interview with Gladstone Wilson, Kingston, Jamaica, June, 1987.

Chapter Six

[1]For example, in 1988, 65 records from Martinique and Guadeloupe were produced for the Christmas and Carnival period and as many were released only six months later for the vacation period.

[2]This paper is based on several years of research in the region. The study of *zouk* music, in particular, was the main focus of two field trips covering seven months between 1987 and 1988. The research was conducted in Martinique, Guadeloupe, St. Lucia, and Dominica because of their geographic, cultural, and musical proximity and their continuous interaction. From a cultural and musical standpoint, Haiti and French Guyana, both with Creole-speaking populations that are probable listeners of *zouk* music, should also have been included in this study. But the political unrest in Haiti and the geographic distance of French Guyana from the four Creole-speaking countries mentioned above prevented their inclusion.

[3]Throughout this paper, the term Creole refers to the French Creole language— for a few decades now, linguistically recognized as a language of its own—spoken in St. Lucia, Dominica, Martinique, Guadeloupe, Guyana, and Haiti.

[4]An agreement among European countries to permit free travel and employment for all countries party to the agreement.

[5]The following approach is a revised version of Frith's theoretical model for the study of aesthetics in popular music (1987).

[6]"Soundscape" is a term used to refer to the sounds that are part of the environment through mass media, migration patterns, and folk traditions.

[7]When there are chart lists, there are made up after disc jockeys on the station check with each other to determine what they played most often during the week.

[8]*Le Monde* (18 May 1987) reported that in a parlimentary report, Michel Pelchat, member of the *Union des Français* (Republican party) from Esonne, responsible for describing the situation of the mass media in the French overseas departments, opposed the development of private radio stations that he judged to be "too numerous and anarchic" on the FM band. (It should be noted that the official number of private radio stations cited here does not include several pirate stations that exist in the islands.)

[9]The figure for the number of radio stations in Guadeloupe comes from the last survey made in March 1988 by the Service de Presse de la Préfecture de la Guadeloupe. The report on the number of radio stations in Martinique was taken from a study made in July 1984 and published in the *Journal Officiel de la Ré*publique Française no. 47: 2451-2452, 24 February 1985.

[10]Soca is an outgrowth of calypso, evolving in the late 1970s.

[11]For further information on migration patterns, see Carnegie 1981, 1987.

[12]I owe this information to two specialists in Latin music who are both announcers at Radio Caraïbe International: Ignace from Martinique and Maxo from Guadeloupe.

[13]The tern *cadence* refers in fact to cadence-rampa, a dance originally from Haiti and attributed to the leading musician Webert Sicot (Renard 1981). More details on this music will be given in the author's forthcoming book on the *zouk* phenomenon.

[14]For further information on the musical traditions of this region, see Crowley, 1955, 1958a, 1958b; Dauphin 1980, 1983a, 1983b; Dauphin and Dévieux 1985; Daryl 1987; Desroches 1985, Gallo 1979; Guilbault 1985, 1987a, 1987b, 1987c; Honorat 1955; Honychurch 1984; Jackson 1985; Jallier 1985; Lafontaine 1982, 1983, 1986; Marcel-Dubois and Pichonnet-Andral 1982; Rosemain 1986; and Saint Cyr 1981.

[15]Many other *zouk* groups exist in the French islands, but none is as successful or influential as Kassav, and none has yet developed the strategies to plan the overall production and distribution of its products to the degree to which Kassav has succeeded.

[16]In a personal communication with the author.

[17]Before the advent of Kassav, the poet and artist Jobby Bernabé from Martinique had already begun such work. Today, he is still considered one of the most inspiring leaders in exploiting the linguistic beauties of Creole.

[18]For the minority groups living in France, *zouk* canalizes energy in relations with the dominant European groups.

[19]Free translation by the author.

[20]It should be noted that the brass section in *zouk* music rarely backs up the chorus, unlike calypso and late 1970s Haitian arrangements of *cadence-rampa*.

[21]This description pertains especially to the fast *zouk* called locally " *zouk* hard." The *"zouk* love, or slower versions with a less marked beat, can actually be built on a verse—refrain pattern.

[22]Simon Frith's expression "possessing [the song]" (1987, p. 143) is, I think, one of the most appropriate ways to describe the double bind that music creates for the listener.

[23]The musicians of Kassav rely on traditional music to make contact with people, but they are not prisoners of its formulas. As the musician Eric Nabajoth (1988) has pointed out, Kassav has brought together many elements in *zouk* that contrast strongly with traditional music, namely,the amplification of the voice through a sound system, the use of brass and technological equipment (such as the rhythm box and synthesizers), the use of sound effects and color changes, the funky style of playing, etc. These elements will be examined in greater detail elsewhere.

[24]Its success is attributed to the fact that African music today is deeply influenced by *zouk* music and borrows many of its characteristics.

[25]The fact that the Caribbean airline Liat has offered cheaper airfare packages for travel within the Caribbean has certainly contributed to this new trend, but cannot totally account for the new interest of French islanders to visit their neighbors. Airfares to Europe have always been more costly than those to neighboring islands, but this has never prevented Guadeloupeans and Martiniquais from travelling to European countries.

[26]This observation comes from the insightful comments of the editor of *Gwan Moun* from Guadeloupe, Danik Zandwonis, during a personal interview.

Chapter Eight

[1]Lapsed literacy results from school attendance and early school leaving patterns of many rural people. Children are kept from school periodically to assist on farms, thereby missing essential lessons and reinforcement of acquired skills. Many leave

school early to work and seemingly lose their literacy skills after long periods without exposure to print materials.

[2]Radio Jamaica Rediffusion (RJR) was purchased by the government in 1977 and is no longer privately owned and operated.

[3]Adapted from Johns Hopkins University (1987) and interviews with Elaine Perkins conducted by Maisha Hazzard, December 1986.

[4]Premeditated sexual activity is implied in preparation for sexual intimacy. According to Perkins, spontaneous involvement seemed more easily condoned as a result of the moment. Young women considering themselves to be "good girls" seemed especially prone to avoid preparation despite pressures by males for sexual intimacy and the numerous examples of the results of "un-premeditated" sexual involvements.

[5]Traditional health attendants often predict the number of children a woman is fated to have by counting the knots on the umbilical cord at the time of delivery; hence, there is often the belief that a woman is destined to give birth to a prescribed number of children.

[6]The Sistrens is a theater cooperative in Kingston dedicated to psychodrama and sociodrama. It is designed to help women develop more self esteem, identify goals and objectives for self development and independence, and work through personal trauma.

Chapter Nine

[1]As of January 1988, Radio France Outre mer had a staff of 92 employees, which included 14 journalists working for the radio and television stations. RCI has three full time journalists, seven free lancers, and eight hosts for music and talk shows. All of these people are paid (Interview, Marival, 1988).

[2]Quotations taken from the Sunday morning news analysis and talk show "Kaw ka di de sa?" *Radyo Tanbou*, 3 January 1988. Creole spelling is based on the work by H. Poullet, S. Telchid, and D. Montbrand (1984).

[3]The way the unpopular tax increase in Moule was presented by the station is an excellent example of their investigative journalistic techniques: A 30-minute news bulletin at 6h30, Friday, 8 January 1988; a discussion on the 12h30 bulletin. Tuesday, 5 January 1988; "Kaw ka di de sa?" a program of commentary, analysis, and phone—in, spent almost an hour on the question, Sunday, 3 January 1988.

References

Abrahams, Roger. 1983. *Man-of-Words in the West Indies: Performance and the Emergence of Creole Culture.* Baltimore: Johns Hopkins University Press.

Althusser, L. 1971. "Ideology and Ideological State Apparatuses." In *Lenin and Philosophy and Other Essays,* translated by R. Brewster, pp. 127-186. New York: Monthly Review Press.

Anderson, Elijah. 1976. *A Place on the Corner.* Chicago: University of Chicago Press.

Antigua Barbuda Department of Statistics. 1985. *Statistical Yearbook.* St. John's, Antigua: Statistical Office, Ministry of Finance.

Axthelm, Pete. 1971. *The City Game: Basketball in New York.* New York: Pocket Books.

Babcock-Abrahams, Barbara. 1975. " 'A Tolerated Margin of Mess': The Trickster Reconsidered." *Journal of the University of Indiana Folk Institute.* V. 11, pp. 147—186.

Babel-Gisler, D. 1981. *La langue créole, force jugulée.* Paris: L'Harmattan.

Balibar, R. and D. Laporte. 1974. *Le Français national.* Paris: Hachette.

Barbu, Z. 1976. "Popular Culture: A Sociological Approach." In *Approaches to Popular Culture,* edited by C.W.E. Bigsby, pp. 39-68. London: Edward Arnold.

Beckford, George and Michael Witter. 1980. *Small Garden, Bitter Weed: The Political Economy of Struggle and Change in Jamaica.* Morant Bay: Maroon Publishing House.

Bellman, Beryl L. 1984. *The Language of Secrecy; Symbols and Metaphors in Poro Ritual.* New Brunswick, New Jersey: Rutgers University Press.

Bickerton, Derek. 1975. *Dynamics of a Creole System.* Cambridge: Cambridge University Press.

Blanchard, Kendall. 1981. *Mississippi Choctaws at Play: The Serious Side of Leisure.* Urbana: University of Illinois Press.

Brodber, Erna and Edward Green. 1981. "Reggae and Cultural Identity in Jamaica." ISER, Series C, No. 7.

Burton, Richard. 1985. "Cricket, Carnival, and Street Culture in the Caribbean." *The British Journal of Sports History,* 2, pp. 179-197.

Carmody, Caroline. 1978. "First Among Equals: Antiguan Patterns of Local-Level Leadership." Ph.D. dissertation, New York University.

Carnegie, Charles V. 1981. "Human Maneuver, Option-Building and Trade: An Essay on Caribbean Social Organization." Unpublished dissertation.

———. 1987. "A Social Psychology of Caribbean Migrations: Strategic Flexibility in the West Indies." In *The Caribbean Exodus,* edited by Barry B. Levine, pp. 32-43. New York: Praeger.

Cohen, Abner. 1974. *Two Dimensional Man: An Essay on Power and Symbolism in Complex Society.* Berkeley: University of California Press.

_____ 1980. "Drama and Politics in the Development of a London Carnival." *Man* (n.s.) 15, pp. 65-87.

Crowley, Daniel. 1955. "Festivals of the Calendar in St. Lucia." *Caribbean Quarterly.* 4(2), pp. 99-121.

_____ 1958a. "The Shak-Shak in the Lesser Antilles." *Ethnomusicology.* 2, pp. 112-115.

_____ 1958b. "La Rose and La Marguerite Societies in St. Lucia." *Journal of American Folklore.* 71, pp. 541-552.

DaBreo, D. Sinclair. 1988. *Will Insularity and Political Opportunism Defeat Caribbean Integration?* Castries, St. Lucia: Commonwealth Publishers International Ltd.

DaMatta, Roberto. 1977. "Constraint and License: Preliminary Study of Two Brazilian National Rituals." In *Secular Ritual,* edited by Sally Moore and Barbara G. Meyerhof. Amsterdam: Van Gorcum and Co. B.V.

_____ 1984. "On Carnival, Informality, and Magic: A Point of View From Brazil." In *Text, Play, and Story.* Edward Bruner (ed.). Washington D.C.: AES.

Dauphin, Claude. 1980. "La Mérinque entre l'Oralité et l'Ecriture: Histoire d'un Genre Musical Haïtien." *Revue de Musique des Universités Canadiennes.* 1, pp. 49—65.

_____ 1983a. *La Chanson Haïtienne Folklorique et Classique.* Montréal: Société de Recherche et de Diffusion de la Musique Haïtienne.

_____ 1983b. *Traité d'Organologie Haïtienne.* Montréal: Université de Montreal.

Demas, William G. 1974. *West Indian Nationhood and Caribbean Integration.* Barbados: CCC Publishing House.

_____ 1988. *Towards O. E. C. S. Political Union.* No publisher listed.

Desroches, Monique. 1985. *La Musique Traditionnelle de la Martinique.* Rapport No. 8. Montréal: Centre de Recherche Caraïbes, Université de Montréal.

Dyde, Brian. 1986. *Antigua and Barbuda: The Heart of the Caribbean.* London: Macmillan.

Eichberg, Henning. 1984. "Olympic Sport: Neocolonization and Its Alternatives." *International Review for the Sociology of Sport,* 19:1.

Evans, Luther H. 1945. *The Virgin Islands: From Naval Base to New Deal.* Ann Arbor: J. W. Edwards.

Farrugia, Pepin et al. 1987. "Débat sur l'Europe." *Grin Fos/Grain de Force* (Basse-Terre, Guadeloupe), no. 2, pp. 25-30.

Foner, Nancy. 1985. "Race and Color: Jamaican Migrants in London and New York City." *International Migration Review.* 19, pp. 708-727.

Forrestor, C. 1977. *The Role of the Government Information Service.* Mona: Caribbean Institute for Mass Communications, University of the West Indies. Unpublished paper.

Frith, Simon. 1987. "Towards an Aesthetic of Popular Music." In *Music and Society,* edited by Richard Leppert and Susan McClary, pp. 133-149. Cambridge: Cambridge University Press.

Gallo, William. 1979. "Creole Music and Dance in Martinique." *Review Inter—americana.* 8, pp. 666-670.

Genovese, Eugene. 1974. *Roll Jordon Roll: The World the Slaves Made.* New York: Pantheon.

Girvan, N., R. Bernal and W. Hughes. 1980. "The IMF and the Third World: The Case of Jamaica, 1974-80." No. 2. No place of publication given.

Green, Richard. 1986. *Latin America and Caribbean Review.* Essex, England: Middle East Review Co. Ltd.

Gruneau, Richard. 1983. *Class, Sport and Social Development.* Amherst: University of Massachusetts Press.

Guilbault, Jocelyne. 1985. "St. Lucian Kwadril Evening." *Latin American Music Review.* 6:1, pp. 31-57.

———. 1987a. "Fitness and Flexibility: Funeral Wakes in St. Lucia, West Indies." *Ethnomusicology.* 31:2, pp. 273-299.

———. 1987b. "The La Rose and La Marguerite Organizations in St. Lucia: Oral and Literate Strategies in Performance." *Yearbook for Traditional Music.* 19, pp. 97-115.

———. 1987c. *Instruments Musicaux à Ste. Lucie: Contextes d'Apparition et Transmission d'un Savoir Culturel.* Paris: Agence de Coopération Culturelle et Technique.

Guttman, Allen. 1978. *From Ritual to Record: The Nature of Modern Sports.* New York: Columbia University Press.

Hall, S. and P. Whannel. 1965. *The Popular Arts.* New York: Pantheon.

Hector, Tim. 1988. Editorial, *Outlet.* St. John's, Antigua.

Heeger, Gerald A. 1974. *The Politics of Underdevelopment.* New York: St. Martin's Press, Inc.

Henry, Frances. 1987. "Caribbean Migration to Canada: Prejudice and Opportunity." In *The Caribbean Exodus,* edited by Barry B. Levine, pp. 214-222. New York: Praeger.

Henry, Paget. 1983a. "Decolonization and the Authoritarian Context of Democracy in Antigua." In *The Newer Caribbean: Decolonization, Democracy and Development.* Paget Henry and Carl Stone (eds.). Philadelphia: Institute for the Study of Human Issues.

———. 1983b. "Decolonization and Cultural Underdevelopment in the Commonwealth Caribbean." In *The Newer Caribbean: Decolonization, Democracy, and Development,* edited by Paget Henry and Carl Stone, pp. 95-120. Philadelphia: Institute for the Study of Human Issues.

———. 1985. *Peripheral Capitalism and Underdevelopment in Antigua, West Indies.* New Brunswick, N.J.: Transaction Books.

Herskovits, Melville. 1941. *The Myth of the Negro Past.* New York: Harper and Brothers.

Hill, Donald. 1981. "New York's Caribbean Carnival." *Everybody's.* August-September, pp. 33-37.

Hill, Donald and Robert Abramson. 1979. "West Indian Carnival in Brooklyn." *Natural History.* August-September, pp. 73-85.

Hill, Errol. 1972. *The Trinidad Carnival: Mandate for a National Theatre.* Austin: University of Texas Press.

Honorat, Michel Lamartinière. 1955. *Les danses folkloriques Haïtiennes.* Port-au-Prince. No publisher listed.

Honychurch, Lennox. 1984. *The Dominica Story: A History of the Island.* Dominica: The Dominica Institute. First publication, 1975.

Hosein, Everold N. 1975. "Mass Media Preferences, Mass Media Credibility and CARICOM Awareness in Urban St. Lucia." *Caribbean Monthly Bulletin.* July, pp. 14-20.

Howe, Darcus. 1976. "Is a Police Carnival." *Race Today.* 8, pp. 173-175.

Jackson, Irene V., ed. 1985. *More Than Dancing: Essays on Afro-American Music and Musicians.* Westport: Greenwood Press.

Jackson, Marni. 1987. "Mas' Appeal." *Canadian Art.* Summer, pp. 70-77.

Jallier, Maurice and Yollen Lossen. 1985. *Musique aux Antilles: Mizik bò kay*. Paris: Editions Caribbéennes.

Jamaica Journal. 1983. "Current State of Copyright Legislation in Jamaica: Heather Royes Talks to Tom Tavares-Finson, Chairman of the Copyright Commission." 16:1 (February), pp. 14-18.

Jeanne, M. 1981. "Entretien avec Max Jeanne." In *Les Antilles dans l'impasse*, edited by A. Brossat and D. Maragnes, pp. 129-135. Paris: Editions Caribbéennes.

The Johns Hopkins University-Population Information Program. 1987. *Report on Radio Soap Opera Scriptwriters Seminar at the Normendie Hotel, St. Ann's, Trinidad*. Baltimore: The Johns Hopkins University-Population Information Program.

Kaplan, S.L. 1984. *Understanding Popular Culture*. Berlin: Mouton.

Kincaid, Jamaica. 1988. *A Small Place*. New York: Farrar, Strauss, Giroux.

Kirshenblatt-Gimblett, Barbara. 1983. "The Future of Folklore Studies in America." *Folklore Forum*. 16, pp. 175-233.

Knud-Hansen, Knud. 1947. *From Denmark to the Virgin Islands*. Philadelphia: Dorrance and Company.

Lafontaine, Marie-Céline. 1982a. "Musique et Société aux Antilles."*Présence Africaine*. 121/122, pp. 72-108.

_____. 1982b. "Musique et Société aux Antilles: 'Balakadri' ou le Bal de Quadrille au Commandement de la Guadeloupe." *Présence Africaine*. 121/122, pp. 72-108.

_____. 1983. "Le Carnaval de l' 'Autre': A Propos d' 'Authenticite' en Matière de Musique Guadeloupéenne, Théories et Réalités."*Les Temps Modernes*, pp. 2124-2173.

_____. 1986. *Carnot par Lui—même: Alors ma Chère, Moi....* Paris: Editions Caribbéennes.

L'indepéndans. 1986. "Radyo Tanbou: Radio libre la plus écoutée." Août, p. 4.

Little, Kenneth. 1965. "The Political Function of the Poro." *Africa, Journal of the International African Institute* (Vol. 35 (4).

Lowenthal, L. 1961. *Literature, Popular Culture, and Society*. Englewood Cliffs, N.J.: Prentice Hall.

Lynn, W. 1981. "Towards an Integrated Communications Strategy in Support of National Development Community Media: A Jamaica Case Study." Master's thesis, American University.

Mrs. Lanaghan. 1844. *Antigua and the Antiguans*. London: Saunders and Otley.

Manning, Frank. 1973. *Black Clubs in Bermuda: Ethnography of a Play World*. Ithaca: Cornell University Press.

_____. 1977. "Cup Match and Carnival: Secular Rites of Revitalization in Decolonizing Tourist-Oriented Societies." In *Secular Rituals*. Sally Moore and Barbara G. Meyerhof (eds.). Amsterdam: Van Gorcum and Company B.V.

_____. 1978. "Carnival in Antigua (Caribbean Sea): An Indigenous Festival in a Tourist Economy."*Anthropos*. 73, pp. 191-204.

_____. 1982. *Carnival in Canada*. Videotape.

_____. 1983. "Carnival and the West Indian Diaspora." *The Round Table*. April, pp. 186-196.

Marcell-Dubois, Claudie and Maguy Pichonnet—Andral. 1982.*La Musique à Marie-Galante*. Paris: Musée National des Arts et Traditions Populaires, ATP 82, LP 33.

McElroy, Jerome L. and Klaus de Albuquerque. 1984. "Federal Perceptions and Policy Versus Virgin Islands Reality." *The Review of Regional Studies*. 14, pp. 47-55.

Midgett, Douglas. 1982. *Distorted Development: The Resuscitation of the Antiguan Sugar Industry*. Institute of Urban and Regional Research, University of Iowa.

———. 1987. "Industrial Relations, Politics and Labour Legislation in Antigua." *New West Indian Review*. pp 43.49.

Nabajoth, Eric. 1988. "Musique Populaire et Création Artistique." Paper presented at Symposium Kassav sur le *zouk*, Pointe-à-Pitre, Guadeloupe, 25 August.

Naipaul, V.S. 1969. *The Mimic Man*. Hammondsworth: Penguin Publishers.

Nettleford, Rex. 1988. "Implications for Caribbean Development." In *Caribbean Festival Arts*, edited by John W. Nunley and Judith Bettelheim, pp. 183-197. Seattle: University of Washington Press.

Nunley, John W. 1988. "Festival Diffusion into the Metropole." In *Caribbean Festival Arts*, edited by John W. Nunley and Judith Bettelheim, pp. 165-181. Seattle: University of Washington Press.

Orie, Dana. 1987. "Don't Blame the Movements for Carnival Saturday Night." *The Daily News*. 11 May, p. 6.

Ostry, Bernard. 1978. *The Cultural Connection*. Toronto: McClelland and Stewart.

Pearse, Andrew. 1971. "Carnival in Nineteenth Century Trinidad." In *Peoples and Cultures of the Caribbean*, edited by Michael M. Horowitz, Garden City, N.Y.: Natural History Press.

Pereira, Beverley. 1985/86. "Copyright in Jamaica." *Jamaica Library Association Bulletin*, pp. 36-39.

Perkins, Elaine. 1987a. Transcripts of audiotape of Elaine Perkins' presentation to students and faculty, School of Telecommunications, Ohio University, Athens, Ohio, May 1-2.

———. 1987b. *Trip Report: Radio Soap Opera for the Eastern Caribbean, Trinidad and Tobago*, November 23-27, 1987. Unpublished report to the Johns Hopkins University—Population Information Program. Kingston, Jamaica.

Poullet, B., S. Telchid and D. Monbrand. 1984. *Dictionnaire créole-français*. Fort-de-France: Hatier Antilles.

Prince, Althea. 1984. "Anansi Folk Culture: An Expression of Caribbean Life." *Caribbean Review*. Winter, v. XIII(1).

Reisman, Karl. 1974. "Noise and Order." In *Language and Its Social Setting*, edited by William Gage. Washington, D.C.: Anthropological Society of Washington.

Renard, Yves. 1981. "Kadans: Musique Populaire de la Caraïbe Créolophone, Facteur d'Intégration Régionale?" Paper presented at Third International Colloquium on Creole Studies, St. Lucia, May 3-9.

Richards, Novelle. 1981. *The Struggle and the Conquest*, v. II. St. John's, Antigua: Benjie's.

Richards, Vince. 1983. "Decolonization in Antigua: Its Impact on Agriculture and Tourism." In *The Newer Caribbean, Decolonization and Development*, Paget Henry and Carl Stone (eds.). Philadelphia: Institute for the Study of Human Issues.

Richardson, Bonham. 1983. *Caribbean Migrants: Environment and Human Survival in St. Kitts and Nevis*. Knoxville: University of Tennessee Press.

Rosemain, Jacqueline. 1986. *La Musique dans la Société Antillaise 1635-1902*. Paris: L'Harmattan.

Saint Cyr, Jean. 1981. "La Méringue Haïtienne." *Instituo Interamericano de Ethnomusicologica.* 5, pp. 62-74.

Scott, James C. 1972. *Comparative Political Corruption.* Englewood Cliffs, N.J.: Prentice-Hall, Inc.

Segal, Aaron. 1987. "The Caribbean Exodus in a Global Context: Comparative Migration Experiences." In *The Caribbean Exodus*, edited by Barry B. Levine, pp. 44-64. New York: Praeger.

Stewart, John. 1986. "Patronage and Control in the Trinidad Carnival." In *The Anthropology of Experience*, edited by Victor Turner and Edward Bruner, pp. 289-315. Urbana: University of Illinois Press.

Stinner, William, Klaus de Albuquerque and Roy Bryce—Laporte. 1982. *Return Migration and Remittances: Developing a Caribbean Perspective.* Washington, D.C.: RIIES Occasional Paper No. 3, Smithsonian Institution.

Stuckey, Sterling. 1987. *Slave Culture in America: Nationalist Theory and the Foundations of Black America.* New York: Oxford University Press.

Sutton, Constance. 1987. "The Caribbeanization of New York City and the Emergence of a Transnational Sociocultural System." In *Caribbean Life in New York City: Sociocultural Dimensions*, edited by Constance Sutton and Elsa Chaney, pp. 15—30. New York: Center for Migration Studies.

Thompson, Robert. 1988. "Recapturing Heaven's Glamour: Afro—Caribbean Festivalizing Arts." In *Caribbean Festival Arts*, edited by John Nunley and Judith Bettelheim, pp. 17-29. Seattle: University of Washington Press.

UNESCO. 1985. *Statistical Yearbook.* Paris: UNESCO.

United Nations Industrial Development Organization. 1987. *Industrial Development Review Series: The Caribbean Region.* Vienna: United Nations Industrial Development Organization.

Walcott, Derek. 1973. "Meanings." In *Consequences of Class and Color: West Indian Perspectives*, edited by David Lowenthal and Lambros Comitas, pp. 302-312. New York: Anchor Books.

Wallerstein, Immanuel. 1974-1980. *The Modern World System.* New York: Academic Press.

Waters, Anita. 1985. *Race, Class and Political Symbols: Rastafari and Reggae in Jamaican Politics.* New Brunswick, N.J.: Transaction.

Wiggins, William. 1987. *O Freedom!: Afro-American Emancipation Celebrations.* Knoxville: University of Tennessee Press.

Wilson, Peter. 1973. *Crab Antics: The Social Anthropology of English Speaking Negroes in the Societies of the Caribbean.* New Haven: Yale University Press.

Interviews

Decrozes, Jacques Barbier, regional director of RFO, by Alvina Ruprecht, Pointe-à-Pitre, Guadeloupe, November 28, 1987.

Eccles, Clancy, Jamaican entertainer, by Gladstone Wilson, Kingston, Jamaica, 1987.

Khan, Rafiq, UNESCO advisor, Jamaica, by Vibert Cambridge, May 1988.

Marival, Daniel, information editor of RCI, by Alvina Ruprecht, Gosier, Guadeloupe, January 8, 1988.

Mekel Barbotteau, Alexyna (Ernestine), journalist for Radyo Tanbou, by Alvina Ruprecht, Pointe-à-Pitre, Guadeloupe, December 30, 1987.

Melhado, O.K., by Gladstone Wilson, Kingston, Jamaica, 1987.

Patterson, P.J., by Gladstone Wilson, Kingston, Jamaica, 1987.

Perkins, Elaine, radio personality, by Maisha Hazzard, in Kingston, Jamaica, 1986.

Contributors

Vibert Cambridge is a doctoral student in the School of Telecommunications, Ohio University. Previous to that, he held many positions in his native Guyana.

Marlene Cuthbert is professor of communication and chair of graduate studies, Department of Communication Studies, University of Windsor. Her research on the Caribbean focuses on communication technology, dependency and development, cultural policy, and the recording industry and youth.

Klaus de Albuquerque is professor of sociology and anthropology at the College of Charleston. He has lived and worked in the Caribbean on and off since 1970, and has published extensively on intro-Caribbean migration, crime, urbanization, Caribbean development, and tourism. He has been the recipient of numerous grant awards to do research in the region.

Jocelyne Guilbault, an ethnomusicologist at the Music Department, University of Ottawa, has carried out extensive research on traditional music in both the French-and English-speaking Caribbean. Her work has been published extensively, including in *Ethnomusicology Review, Latin American Music Review*, and *Yearbook of Traditional Music*.

Maisha L. Hazzard is on the faculty of the School of Telecommunications, Ohio University. She has presented the findings of her research on Jamaica and Guyana at national conferences.

John A. Lent, director of Third World Media Associates (669 Ferne Blvd., Drexel Hill, Pa. 19026), has carried out research on Caribbean mass communications since 1968. He has published numerous books and articles on the topic, including *Third World Mass Media and Their Search for Modernity: The Case of Commonwealth Caribbean, 1717-1976; Caribbean Mass Communications: A Comprehensive Bibliography*; and *Mass Communications in the Caribbean*.

Jay R. Mandle is Professor of Economics and History at Temple University.

Joan D. Mandle is Associate Professor of Sociology at Penn State University. A different version of this article was published in *Grass Roots Commitment: Basketball and Society in Trinidad and Tobago*. Parkersberg, Iowa: Caribbean Books, 1988.

Frank Manning has written widely on Caribbean entertainment, festivity, sport, religion, and politics. He is author of *Black Clubs in Bermuda*, editor of *The Celebration of Society* and *The World of Play*, and general editor of the *Culture and Performance* book series. He is professor of anthropology and director of the Centre for Social and Humanistic Studies, University of Western Ontario.

Alvina Ruprecht is assistant professor of French at Carleton University, Ottawa. She also reviews theatre for the English and French language services of the Canadian Broadcasting Company. She has published analyses of various aspects of the French language press of Quebec, French Caribbean, and France, as well as articles on dramatic discourse and contemporary Quebec dramaturgy.

Inga Treitler is a doctoral candidate in anthropology at the University of Illinois. Her dissertation research focuses on political discourse in Antigua, using analytical methods from cognitive and symbolic anthropology. Ms. Treitler is a recent recipient of a Fulbright grant and will be spending the next year in Antigua continuing her research.

Gladstone Wilson has been a journalist in Jamaica for over twenty years. A former president of the Press Association of Jamaica, Wilson helped launch *Camwork*, a regional mass communications organization in the Caribbean. He has carried out primary research on a number of topics, including popular culture, and finished a master's in communications at the University of Windsor.

DATE DUE

FEB 2 1 1995	
DEC 1 2 2005	